FORGIVEN AND NOT FORGOTTEN

How God used one woman's life to bring revelation of what He is doing in this present darkness

By Terra Kern

Higher Ground Books & Media
Springfield, Ohio.
http://highergroundbooksandmedia.com

Printed in the United States of America 2020

PREFACE

In times of prayer, meditation and reflection, God kept bringing back to my memory my childhood and how I learned of Him, talked with Him, and all the times throughout my life when I experienced angelic activity, and of times I was led by the Holy Spirit. He reminded me of how He had never left nor forsaken me, of how intimately He knew and loved me and provided for me. He reminded me of the times I prayed and He answered, the times He spoke to me, the times He led and called me into intercessory prayer and taught me about spiritual warfare and of the times I experienced supernatural manifestations throughout my life.

I heard the Spirit say, "Write down the things I show you. Write down how I have been with you since the days of your youth, how I have held you and kept you and loved you throughout your life and put them in a book. They will serve as examples and will be the words of your testimony."

This brought me to my knees in reverent prayer, brought about searching scriptures and many more hours of prayer and seeking His will and direction. In doing so, three main areas became prevalent, those being children/youth, angels, and supernatural manifestations. For months He began to open up the Scriptures pertaining to the times we are in and bring the light of revelation to them in a way I had not understood before.

I sense the Spirit saying that God is ushering in a new thing for this present day, a great move and outpouring of his Spirit for the present darkness, the present course of this world this generation finds itself in. That He is beginning to pour fresh anointing upon his church, the body of Christ, and the gates of Hell will not prevail against it.

From the very beginning, before He even laid out the foundation of the earth, God has had a plan for each and every one of us concerning His kingdom. From the Old Testament through the New, God has been revealing His plan to us concerning His church, and for over 2000 years, Christ has been building it.

It is in gross darkness that light shines brightest. I hear the Spirit saying in this present move of God, there will be an increase in the level of anointing upon His church, the body of Christ, including upon our children and youth. There will be an increase in angelic activity, as well as an increase in supernatural manifestations so that multitudes will lovingly be led out of the darkness into his glorious light. It is the beginning of His culmination.

It is my prayer that throughout this book, your focus be solely on God; God the father, God the Son, and God the Holy Spirit.

John1:14 "And the Word became flesh and dwelt among us..."

John1:1- 5 "In the beginning was the Word, and the Word was with God, and the Word was God. He was in the beginning with God. All things were made through Him, and without Him nothing was made that was made. In Him was life, and the life was the light of men. And the light shines in the darkness, and the darkness did not comprehend it."

John 16:13 "However, when He, the Spirit of truth, has come, He will guide you into all truth; for He will not speak on His own authority, but whatever He hears He will speak; and He will tell you things to come."

First Timothy 4:1-5 KJV "Now the Spirit speaketh expressly, that in the latter times some shall depart from the faith, giving heed to seducing spirits, and doctrines of devils; speaking lies in hypocrisy; having their conscience seared with a hot iron; forbidding to marry, and commanding to abstain from meats, which God hath created to be received with thanksgiving of them which believe and know the truth. For every creature of God is good, and nothing to be refused, if it be received with thanksgiving: For it is sanctified by the word of God and prayer."

Second Timothy 3:1-5 "But know this, that in the last days perilous times will come: For men will be lovers of themselves, lovers of money, boasters, proud, blasphemers, disobedient to parents, unthankful, unholy, unloving, unforgiving, slanderers, without self-control, brutal, despisers of good, having a form of godliness but denying its power..."

Second Timothy 4:3-4 "For the time will come when they will not endure sound doctrine, but according to their own desires, because they have itching ears, they will heap up for themselves teachers; and they will turn their ears away from the truth, and be turned aside to fables."

Acts 2:17-19 And it shall come to pass in the last days, says God, That I will pour out of My Spirit on all flesh; Your sons and your daughters shall prophesy, Your young men shall see visions,

Your old men shall dream dreams. And on my menservants and on my maidservants, I will pour out My Spirit in those days; and they shall prophesy, I will show wonders in heaven above and signs in the earth beneath…

First Corinthians 13:13 …but the greatest of these is love.

CHAPTER ONE
LET THE LITTLE CHILDREN COME TO ME

Around and around I spun myself in the front yard, down the driveway, and into the road with arms outstretched and fingers spread wide, enjoying the air that rushed between my fingers and all around me. Why? The answer is quite simple. It is because I wanted to dance and play with God. Mom explained to me that Father God is Spirit and is everywhere on the earth, in the air around us, and up in heaven. She told me God knew everything and everyone because He created everything and everyone, including me.

All I wanted to do was feel him and let Him know that I knew He was there as much as He knew I was there. I wanted Him to know that I knew He loved me and that I loved Him right back! Ah, the sweet innocence and faith of a little child. Such is the kingdom of heaven.

The above is one of the very first memories I have of God, and it would turn out to be the cornerstone of my faith, the very thing that would get me through life's tumultuous and winding road. The very thing that would cover and protect me in a world at times cruel, unfair and undeniably evil, a world I so often couldn't understand.

There were many instances when I was just a mere little thing, in which Mom and Dad would take the opportunity to share with me the things of God and of His Son, Jesus. The very first of which being the Christmas story about the birth of Jesus. Because of those teaching moments, I believed God, Jesus, and the Holy Spirit were as real as you and me, a father, a friend who was always there, always ready to listen and to help. I began talking to God after that and have never stopped.

I remember being in the backseat of the car when all of a sudden there was a loud rolling clap of thunder. From the front seat, Dad said, "Oh, oh! God is angry with someone." My mom followed by saying that if it began to rain, that meant God was sad about it too. I told my mom and dad I knew what God was mad about. I explained that earlier that day, little Jimmy had stolen Dee's digging spoon and wouldn't give it back. Mom and Dad smiled at one another up there in the front seat. Upon seeing that, I was confident I had it right. A few moments later, it began to pour down rain. I understood in that moment that God cared about the very things we did, and He was sad and hurt when people were done wrong, just like me. I really liked God!

Another time, as an Easter gift, Mom gave me a little charm bracelet that had a mustard seed in a clear ball dangling from it. She explained that the mustard seed was an incredibly tiny seed but grew into an extremely large plant. She further explained that it represented faith or belief. She shared with me that Jesus taught although it is the smallest of all seeds, it grows into one of the largest plants and becomes a tree. And if we only have faith the size of this wee mustard seed, we can speak to problems or mountains and make them move out of our way in Jesus' name. I knew I had a lot of belief, way bigger than that tiny mustard seed. I was completely impressed with faith and determined in my heart I would always have it! Although these instances my parents shared with me about God may seem small, they were God seeds planted within me that took root and began to grow.

Allow me to pause there for a moment and backtrack a bit, delving into the word of God pertaining to little children, angels, and supernatural manifestations. At this point, I should explain that "supernatural" is merely being above and beyond that which is natural or is outside of natural law or phenomena. Let's take a look at the Christmas story to set precedence for what the Spirit has been revealing relative to this book. Throughout the entire Christmas story, we find a child, angels, and supernatural manifestations.

Matthew 1:18-21 "Now the birth of Jesus Christ was as follows: After His mother Mary was betrothed to Joseph, before they came together, she was found with child of the Holy Spirit. Then Joseph her husband, being a just man, and not wanting to make her a public example, was minded to put her away secretly. But while he thought about these things, behold, an angel of the Lord appeared to him in a dream, saying, 'Joseph, son of David, do not be afraid to take to you Mary your wife, for that which is conceived in her is of the Holy Spirit. And she will bring forth a Son, and you shall call His name Jesus, for He will save His people from their sins.'"

Luke 2: 6-14 "So it was, that while they were there, the days were completed for her to be delivered. And she brought forth her firstborn Son, and wrapped Him in swaddling cloths, and laid Him in a manger, because there was no room for them in the inn. Now there were in the same country shepherds living out in the fields, keeping watch over their flock by night. And behold, an angel of the Lord stood before them, and the glory of the Lord shone around them, and they were greatly afraid. Then the angel said to them, 'Do not be afraid, for behold, I bring you good tidings of great joy which will be to all people. For there is born to you this day in the city of David a Savior, who is Christ the Lord. And this will be the sign to you: You will find a Babe wrapped in swaddling cloths, lying in a manger.' And suddenly there was with the angel a multitude of the heavenly host praising God and saying: 'Glory to God in the highest, And on earth peace, goodwill toward men!'"

There are many more instances of angels and supernatural manifestations in the account of the birth of Jesus like the star appearing over Bethlehem, however, the above scriptures cover them quite nicely from the beginning to the end. And there you have it. Often, the first Christmas is the first time a child hears of God, Jesus, angels, the Holy Spirit and supernatural manifestations. When we share the account with little children, they accept it as truth. We should not stop there for it is a great springboard from which to begin teaching more of God's Word to them as Scripture instructs us to do.

Deuteronomy 6:6-7 "And these words I command you shall be in your heart. You shall teach them diligently to your children, and shall talk of them when you sit in your house, when you walk by the way, when you lie down, and when you rise up."

Proverbs 22:6 "Train up a child in the way he should go, and when he is old, he will not depart from it."

Ephesians 6:4 "And you, fathers, do not provoke your children to wrath, but bring them up in the training and admonition of the Lord."

These are just a mere sampling from Scripture, but the instruction is clear.

The next memory I have is the summer after I had started going to school. There was a school bus driving in the neighborhood. I found that quite exciting as the only school buses I had seen before were at the school dropping off children who weren't from our neighborhood. I asked one of the bigger kids from down the street what that bus was doing, driving around here. I was told it was the bus that picked up the kids going to Sunday school and taking them to the church. I said that I wanted to go and was told I would have to ask my parents. I ran home and told my mom about it and she told me I could go the next Sunday.

Now, I'm going to be completely open and honest here and tell you the reason I wanted to go was solely because I wanted to ride on a bus. That was it. But I know as sure as I know my name that God was working behind the scenes on my behalf. He had a plan and purpose for me and my life before he even created the foundations of the earth.

Jeremiah 1:5 "Before I formed you in the womb, I knew you: Before you were born, I sanctified you…"

Psalm 139:13-16 "For you formed my inward parts; You covered me in my mother's womb. I will praise You, for I am fearfully and wonderfully made; Marvelous are your works, and that my soul knows very well. My frame was not hidden from You, When I was made in secret, and skillfully wrought in the lowest parts of the earth. Your eyes saw my substance being yet unformed. And in your book, they all were written, the days fashioned for me, when yet there were none of them."

Ephesians 1:4 "Just as he chose us in Him before the foundation of the world…"

Yes, God knew you and me even before he set the foundation of the earth! How awe-inspiring is that?

Sunday rolled around and I was excited. I had a pretty pink dress on as I stood on the side of the road eagerly awaiting the arrival of that bus. It came and my parents watched from the window as I climbed aboard. I waved to them from my seat by the window and I was off. It was great fun riding, stopping to pick up other children, and riding on some more. I learned that day busses were very bumpy.

When we arrived at the church, a lady came up to me and asked me my name and age. Upon telling her, she brought me to a room downstairs and introduced me to the teacher. I had such fun in the class not only learning a Bible story, but then getting to do a craft related to that story. I got some animal crackers and some fruit punch, and I loved the whole thing from beginning to end. I knew I wanted to go again.

When the bus dropped me back off at home, I noticed an older boy from two doors down sitting on our front porch. He was the oldest boy of our family's friends. When he saw me, he stood up and told me I had to come to his house because my family had gone to my grandma's house and they would be back later. I couldn't believe my mom and dad, and my brother and sister had gone without me. I loved visiting my grandma. I started to cry because my feelings were hurt. He told me not to cry, they would be back for me, but in the meantime, I got to come over and play at his house. Eight children lived there, and I always had fun when we visited, so I went with him.

When next Sunday came, my mom asked me if I wanted to go to church again and I hesitated because I didn't want to be excluded from a visit with Grandma again. But there was this unexplainable pull inside of me, drawing me back to the church. I went, fearing I could be left behind again, but wanted to go to church and learn further about God even more than that fear. This was my routine Sunday after Sunday. My older sister, younger brother, and neighbor kids from our friend's house soon joined me and went to Sunday school too. It was there, in that church, I asked Jesus to come live in my heart. I already knew God was all around me and was impressed to learn that His Son could live inside me. I was all in.

Every time I arrived home from Sunday school, I shared the Bible stories I learned with my mom. And I'll never forget the day my mom called me into my room and presented me with my first Bible. She told me since I was going to church, I needed one. The cover of the Bible was a picture of Jesus sitting on a rock with children gathered all around him. The colors were so bright, brilliant and vivid; it is still etched in my memory today. Throughout my Bible, interspersed between the pages, were pictures of men and women in relation to the Scriptures. I loved my Bible and determined I would read it all, from beginning to end.

Of course, I didn't understand most of it, but I sounded out some words I didn't know as best I could so I truly would have read it all. It took me months upon months to finish. Those things I did understand stuck with me and I carried them around in my heart, in my mind and in my spirit. When I came to the pictures though, I sat and gazed at them for quite a while. I remember looking at those pictures one time and telling God that I wanted to be a person just like those men and women. I wanted to do whatever He told me to do, and I meant it deep down in my heart.

Yes, I talked to God and when He talked back, I didn't find it strange at all and just assumed everyone had conversations with Him. It is what He desires and seeks. Just as He walked and talked with Adam and Eve in the garden on a daily basis, He desires to do so with us. He is a God who seeks relationship with us because He loves us.

This was the beginning of my life in God and I am so thankful I had parents who introduced me to my Heavenly Father and taught me of His ways. For throughout my life there would be times when I needed Him greatly and called upon Him in times of trouble. There would be times when I needed a friend to talk to and Jesus was always there to listen and the Holy Spirit there to lead and guide me and teach me of His ways.

It wasn't long before the evil of a fallen world would strike. It started when at the tender age of eight, my parents divorced, and my dad moved out. Shortly thereafter, my mom sold our childhood home and moved us to my grandma's house while we waited for the new house to be move in ready. It was while we were living at my grandma's house that I talked to God about my troubles.

I was in my grandma's bedroom, lying on the foot of her bed crying because I missed my dad so much. I told God that I didn't like this thing called divorce. I then asked Him if I was going to have a husband. I told Him I didn't want one if I was going to get divorced too. He told me that I would have a husband. Then I asked of Him what my husband would be like. God explained to me that he would be a lot like my dad while at the same time, giving me a brief blurry glimpse in a vision of a man who was skinny, had dark hair and hazel colored eyes, just like my dad! God is so awesome and knows us so intimately. He knew that was the very thing that would calm my little heart, for I was a daddy's girl and loved my dad deeply. I thought he was the greatest man on the whole earth and the thought of marrying a man like him elated me.

The hard smacks of a fallen world didn't stop with my parents' divorce. For it was soon followed by my dad's remarrying. Then a year thereafter, being what I felt, was ripped from the arms of my mom. Leaving her and my baby brother and big sister to move in with my dad and stepmom was a devastating blow. Living with my dad and stepmom further would try to hack away at my heart. I was thankful I got to go and be with my mom and sister and brother on the weekends and for the holidays, but for me, I felt it wasn't enough.

Then the day my dad brought home adoption papers for my stepmom to adopt me shattered my heart to smithereens. I was told it was for my own good because if I was seriously hurt, my stepmom wouldn't be able to legally sign for my care. Everybody thought it was for the best, except me. Therefore, I still always referred to her as my stepmom for clarification and my mother, my mom, despite the adoption. Rejection reared its ugly head and infiltrated my tender little heart. For years I begged and pleaded to be allowed to go back and live with my mom, but time and time again, I was denied my request.

On and on the cold brutal punches of a fallen world would wallop and try to destroy me. But God never left me and was with me even during the times I couldn't feel or hear from Him. But oh, the times I could!

My teenage years were turbulent as most are, but the biggest wallop to me came when I went to our pastor and described the abuse I was going through at home. He then requested to speak with my dad and stepmom, and they came away saying the pastor was wrong. Therefore, we didn't return to church after that until that pastor was moved to another church and a new one took his place.

After the failure to get relief from the church I thought would save me, I cried out to God to take my life time and time again. When I say cried, I mean literally. I would lie in my bed and think of how hopeless my life was. I would bawl and wail and moan in deep pain with tears spilling out from my stinging, swollen eyes, saturating my pillow. I told God I didn't want to live anymore. I begged Him to take my life. I blocked the thoughts of suicide though because I knew that was a sin and I didn't want to sin against God, but thought if He took my life, I would still go to heaven.

I explained to my heavenly Father that I was alone and unloved. I explained to Him that my dad didn't love me because if he did, he wouldn't let my stepmom treat me that way, leaving bruises, fat lips, and welts in her wake. Then when she did, just say he was sorry and give me money to buy whatever I wanted. I knew my stepmom didn't love me because when you love someone, you don't beat on them and force them to drink dish soap making them vomit because you didn't like what they said. You can't claim to love me and then turn around and tell your friend that you wish you had never taken me. I told God I knew even my own mom didn't love me because she wouldn't let me come back even though she knew I was unhappy here. That was her promise to me. I explained I knew the common denominator here was me. I knew that I was unlovable. But God would not grant me my prayer. I woke up every morning still breathing and very much alive. Hallelujah! I thank and praise Him for it now.

The above lament of mine of course wasn't "the" truth, but it was "my" truth as I knew it, my perception of the situation gleaned from not having all of the facts at the time. Lies whispered in my ears I unwittingly believed from Satan, the father of all lies. Satan also tried to take advantage of my situation by sending along others to entice me with illicit drugs and other things that hurting and depressed youth fall into, in attempts to self-medicate and numb the pain. Things sought after to make them feel loved when they didn't at home. But the Holy Spirit would speak to me and tell me not to, lest the devil win. He would tell me I was too important and too smart to fall for that. And I never wanted the devil to win in my life! I knew since I was a little girl that my weapon of warfare was bigger than his and that I could beat him.

Allow me to explain. God is so creative and amazing in the ways He chooses to teach us. When my sister and I were little, my mom would read to us. She had a book from her childhood that featured stories from around the world. This particular day, I saw a cartoon picture of the earth with men in suits and top hats on top of the earth and oriental men with thin long mustaches, upside down on the bottom of the earth. I asked my mom what that picture was, and she told my sister and me that China was located below the United States and if we were to dig straight down through the earth, we would be in China.

After story time, my sister and I went outside to play. She asked me if I wanted to dig down to China and I thought going to China would be fun. After going into the garage and getting two of our dad's shovels, we began to dig a hole in the front yard. After we had dug down about a foot and a half, it dawned on me that we would have to dig through hell where the devil lived. We had been taught by our parents that the devil's domain was hell, located in the center of the earth. My sister agreed with me and we began to consider if we should continue.

Right then, the only picture of the devil I had ever seen before, popped into my head. It was the little devil on the can of Underwood Deviled Ham Spread. The little devil was red with horns on its head, had a pointed tail, and was holding a little pitchfork. I thought of my dad's pitchforks in the garage and knew right away they were bigger. I ran into the garage and grabbed them. Holding a pitchfork in each hand, I ran back to my sister in the front yard. I handed one to her and told her we should keep on digging because our pitchforks were bigger than the devil's and we could take him. From that point on, I always knew the devil would not win against me because my weapons were bigger than his. It was just something that I somehow knew deep down in my spirit and never wavered from.

For clarification, I didn't mean to imply that my adolescent years were all dark, for they weren't. I was daddy's girl and loved him dearly and we had plenty of good times together. We fished, we hunted, we went off road in the jeep through the fields, and we went snowmobiling, ice skating, waterskiing, took trips up north, and so much more. I had a lot of friends and friends whose parents adored me. I played sports and was involved in a lot of after school activities. Almost all of my teachers and coaches valued and praised me. I just wanted to highlight the path my life took, the dark forks in the road that slowly veered me down a shadowy alleyway that didn't include me seeking God diligently. That didn't include continuing to talk to Him and consider His ways daily as I had as a child. I slowly but surely drifted away. But He never left me.

Finally, when I was seventeen, I left my dad's house and moved back to my mom's. Mom and I had long discussions together about so many things. We discussed the things I had learned while growing up in the church when I lived with my dad, and what my beliefs were. But the most important discussion we had was in discussing our relationship and our feelings, for we found answers to questions that had plagued both of our hearts for years.

It was then that I discovered the time my mom told me I got to come back to live with her, but was later told she had changed her mind, wasn't true at all. I learned she had always loved me and wanted me to come back. We discovered that my dad had lied to us both. He told me my mom had changed her mind and decided she didn't want me back because I was a difficult child and she didn't think she could handle me. Then he told my mom that I had changed my mind because I didn't think she was a good mother and couldn't financially provide for me all the things my dad could.

All of those years my mom and I had felt rejected and the reason we carried pain in our hearts wasn't even true. Mom and I held each other in our arms, wept, sobbed, and rocked back and forth hugging for hours as healing slowly took over. I am so thankful for that time with my mom, for in a little over three years, I would lose her in a car accident.

I am also grateful for being taught of God's ways when I was just a little one, for they were the very things that took root in my heart and created the solid foundation in my life that I so needed. As Jesus said, "Let the little children come to me, and do not forbid them; for of such is the kingdom of God. Assuredly, I say to you, whoever does not receive the kingdom of God as a little child will by no means enter it." And He took them up in His arms, laid His hands on them, and blessed them. (Mark 10:13-16). God has a heart for children, just as He did for me when I was just a wee little thing.

CHAPTER TWO
AMPLIFIED ANOINTING UPON OUR CHILDREN AND YOUTH

Have you ever wondered why God chose to send Jesus to earth as an infant, a babe, a child? I know this has been pondered upon by many. But don't think it strange, for Jesus was sent not only fully God, but also fully human to experience every situation mankind would ever encounter so that He could know what we go through from infancy on up and be able to understand, help, and intercede for us throughout our lives.

Hebrews 2:17-18 says, "Therefore in all things He had to be made like his brethren, that He might be a merciful and faithful High Priest in things pertaining to God, to make propitiation for the sins of His people. For that in He Himself has suffered, being tempted, He is able to aid those who are tempted." And Hebrews 4:15 says, "For we do not have a High Priest who cannot sympathize with our weaknesses, but was in all points tempted as we are, yet without sin."

We most often think of these verses in relationship to adulthood alone, however, as Paul said in First Corinthians 15:46, first the natural, then the spiritual. When we understand the natural first, we then can understand the spiritual. Jesus came in the natural as an infant, a child, and therefore knows and understands everything about babes, children and youth. He understands the faith of a child. He understands that when children are young, they learn at a faster pace than at any other time in life. He understands their eagerness and hunger to comprehend the world around them. He understands all stages and challenges of childhood just as He understands those of adulthood. There is a distinct purpose for Jesus coming as a babe. So, he could fully understand little ones all the way through their youth, and into and throughout adulthood.

This is why we are instructed to diligently teach our children the Word of God, teach the scriptures as the facts they are right along with all of the other facts and information we give them. Let's take a look at the Scriptures and see what Jesus said regarding little children. In the Book of Matthew, Jesus and His disciples had come into Capernaum and the disciples wanted to know who was greatest in the kingdom of heaven. Matthew 18:2-3 reads, "Then Jesus called a little child to Him, set him in the midst of them, and said,

'Assuredly I say to you, unless you are converted and become as little children, you will by no means enter the kingdom of heaven.'"

Here, Jesus is speaking of the childlike faith we must have in order to enter the kingdom of heaven. He understands the immense faith and complete trust children have. He knows of their simplicity, their unbridled hope, their joy of life itself, their spontaneity, and their faith filled with wide-eyed wonder. He knows they are not shackled by inhibitions. He knows because He was one.

In verse 4, Jesus continues and says, "Therefore whoever humbles himself as this little child is the greatest in the kingdom of heaven." Here, Jesus is teaching that young children are an excellent image of the disciple who is called to follow him with childlike acceptance. He knows about childlike acceptance, because He had been a child.

Then in verse 6, Jesus warns about causing or leading a child to sin. "Whoever causes one of these little ones who believe in Me to sin, it would be better for him if a millstone were hung around his neck, and he were drowned in the depth of the sea." And this is also because of a child's simplicity, their unbridled hope, their joy of life itself, their spontaneity, and their faith filled with wide-eyed wonder. In verse 10 Jesus says, "Take heed that you do not despise one of these little ones, for I say to you that in heaven their angels always see the face of my Father who is in heaven."

Jesus was able to teach about children not only because He had been one, but because we were all one as well and can therefore understand. In the above scriptures Jesus also illustrated us as babes in Christ when we first begin our journey with Him. Again, He was able to do so because He himself had been a little one.

From the above examples of scripture, we can clearly see that Jesus has a heartbeat for children. And so does our Heavenly Lord as Isaiah 54:13 says, "All your children shall be taught by the LORD, and great shall be the peace of your children."

Now let's see what the Bible teaches us about some children and youth who were brought up in the ways of God. We have young Josiah who reigned as king and purged the land of idolatry. Second Chronicles 34:1-3 says, "Josiah was eight years old when he became king, and he reigned thirty-one years in Jerusalem. And he did what was right in the sight of the Lord and walked in the ways of his father David; he did not turn aside to the right hand or to the left. For in the eighth year of his reign, while he was still young, he began to seek the God of his father David; and in the twelfth year he began to purge Judah and Jerusalem of the high places, the wooden images, the carved images, and the molded images."

What about Samuel? Samuel lived in a time when contempt for God's law was commonplace. He eventually became a powerful and influential man, but before that, he was just an inconspicuous student in the temple. You see, when he was just a baby, his mother had dedicated him to God, and therefore Samuel lived in the temple grounds where he was educated. We find Samuel ministered to the Lord even as a child. Then one night while he was still a youngster, something extraordinary happened to him. He heard the word of, and a call from God.

From First Samuel Chapter 3, we learn that God called out to Samuel telling him in verses 11-14 "... Behold, I will do something in Israel at which both ears of everyone who hears it will tingle. In that day I will perform against Eli all that I have spoken concerning his house, from beginning to end. For I have told him that I will judge his house forever for the iniquity which he knows, because his sons made themselves vile, and he did not restrain them. And therefore, I have sworn to the house of Eli that the iniquity of Eli's house shall not be atoned for by sacrifice or offering forever." Then verse 19 reads, "So Samuel grew, and the LORD was with him and let none of his words fall to the ground. And all Israel from Dan to Beersheba knew that Samuel had been established as a prophet of the LORD."

Perhaps the most well-known youth of the Bible is David. The account of David and the giant Goliath has been shared throughout the centuries and holds many lessons. But let's focus on David the adolescent.

During the time of King Saul's reign, there came a time when the Philistines had gathered their armies and were taunting the men of Israel and flaunting their strongest warrior, Goliath, in front of the Israeli army. After a forty-day standoff, the giant Goliath asked, "Why have you come out for battle? Am I not a Philistine and you the servants of Saul? Choose a man for yourselves and let him come down to me. If he is able to fight with me and kill me, then we will be your servants. But if I prevail against him and kill him, then you shall be our servants and serve us. I defy the armies of Israel this day; give me a man that we may fight together." When Saul and all of Israel heard the words of the Philistine, they were dismayed and greatly afraid.

At this time, David was sent by his father Jesse to visit the front lines, bring his brothers food, and bring back battle news from his brothers. David heard Goliath mocking Israel and their God with his taunting and flaunting and volunteered to fight Goliath. This surprised the men of Israel and embarrassed his brothers. His brothers knew him as the boy that kept the sheep, a boy not even old enough to be in the army. But you see, while David was tending the sheep, the Lord Himself had trained David in warfare and had in fact, chosen David to be the one who killed Goliath.

Some men who had heard David, informed Saul about it and Saul therefore sent for David. When David told Saul he would fight the Philistine, Saul responded with, "You are not able to go against this Philistine to fight with him; for you are a youth, and he a man of war from his youth". But David replied, "Your servant used to keep his father's sheep, and when a lion or a bear came and took a lamb out of the flock, I went out after it and struck it, and delivered the lamb from its mouth; and when it arose against me, I caught it by its beard, and struck and killed it. I have killed both the lion and the bear; and this uncircumcised Philistine will be like one of them, seeing he has defied the armies of the living God. The Lord who delivered me from the paw of the lion and bear, He will deliver me from the hand of this Philistine."

Saul consented and David took down Goliath with a stone and a sling. Not the weapons of a soldier in the army, but the weapon he was accustomed to as a shepherd boy in the field coupled with his faith and anointing. God chose David, the most unlikely candidate to defeat the giant as it says in First Corinthians 1:27 KJV "But God hath chosen the foolish things of the world to confound the wise; and God hath chosen the weak things of the world to confound the things which are mighty."

I believe that the Lord, just as He taught David himself, is teaching and training men and women including our youth and raising people up around the globe in their homes. Not in the church or universities, not by man, but by the Almighty God himself. When these believers emerge and start rising up, many will be completely stunned as they will seem as the most unlikely vessel of God but will work wonders in his name just like David did. David had a heart for God, and so do they. They are experiencing spiritual breakthroughs and are rising up all over the face of the earth.

Could the concept of Mark 9:38-40 be a foreshadowing of this? "Now John answered Him, saying, 'Teacher, we saw someone who does not follow us casting out demons in Your name, and we forbade him because he does not follow us.'

But Jesus said, 'Do not forbid him, for no one who works a miracle in My name can soon afterward speak evil of Me. For he who is not against us is on our side.'"

I personally have always had the mindset of pouring into our children everything that we have learned thus far in our lives, based upon the desire I had as a small child to learn more of Him. What a solid foundation set for God to build upon. We should not only teach our children the Bible stories of the great victories in God from the Old and New Testaments, but of the great works and victories that God is doing in the present, in the here and now. We need to present them as the facts that they are and watch and see what God will do with the youth of this generation.

I'm not sure how some of the church got the mindset that little children cannot be taught of the Holy Spirit at a young age. After all, the Holy Spirit was sent to us after Jesus ascended back to heaven. We teach our children of His birth, and of His death and resurrection. Why do we stop short of teaching them of and introducing them to the Holy Spirit whom Jesus sent to us after Him? I can assure you that small children are not too young to comprehend the Holy Spirit.

I taught a youth Friday Night School of the Holy Spirit in our church while the adults attended the adult class. My students ranged in ages six through nine years of age and I can guarantee you, they can understand and hear from the Holy Spirit. One evening after teaching on some of the ways the Holy Spirit can speak to us, I led them all in prayer, asking for God to speak to them through the Holy Spirit. I then asked all of the children to empty their minds and concentrate on what God wanted them to know by the Holy Spirit. I prayed in the Spirit while the children concentrated. All of a sudden, the children were excited and raising their hands as they wanted to share what had just happened.

A little girl had shared to the class how she heard a voice tell her that she didn't have to listen to what the devil told her to do. That she could cut him off just like she could cut off the lights or the TV. Think James 4:7 "...Resist the devil and he will flee from you." One little boy told of how he saw himself, in his head, riding his bike and

Jesus was there running beside him everywhere he went. It didn't matter where he rode. Jesus was by his side everywhere.

After the children shared with me what they experienced, as was customary, we went to the sanctuary at the end of both classes and I was asked to share about the children's class with the adults. I relayed to them of how God had moved in class and the children heard from the Holy Spirit. When service was over the little boy's grandmother came up to me and shared with me how she knew that was indeed God. She explained her grandson had just got a bike for his birthday and rode it all the time from sunup until sundown. She said she had been praying that the Lord be with him while he rode through his neighborhood to keep him safe from harm. God is so marvelous!

Our youth in this generation today are great influencers. They are very passionate about what they believe in and are extremely vocal about those beliefs. Imagine what they can do for the Kingdom of Heaven once they experience and taste the things of God. Satan is aware of this and I believe is why we see such an attack on our youth today. Suicide, depression, violence, drug overdose, gender confusion and the list goes on and on. They are searching, seeking, and desiring in their hearts, the light. They just don't recognize it as that yet.

But praise the Lord, once they taste of the things of God, look out world, and Satan, jump back! Isaiah Chapter 59 says, "When the enemy comes in as a flood, The Spirit of the LORD will lift up a standard against him." Our world is undeniably experiencing the enemy coming in as a flood, so hallelujah and praise the Lord, for He is lifting up a standard even at this moment.

I hear the Spirit of the Lord saying God is bringing us into a new season, a new anointing, and is doing a new thing. And it will include children and youth. Psalm 8:2, "Out of the mouths of babes and nursing infants you have ordained strength because of your enemies, that you may silence the avenger."

CHAPTER THREE
I WILL NOT LEAVE YOU NOR FORSAKE YOU

It wasn't long after moving back with my mom, finishing high school, working a few jobs, and getting some additional education, I had an opportunity arise to leave Michigan and go out and explore and experience our great country. I got to visit states I had never been to before and see some of our great national treasures. I got to visit the ocean for the first time, see the Grand Canyon, experience driving through mountains, and drive through the center of a gigantic Redwood tree. It was exciting, thrilling, and breathtaking. All of these spectacular displays of nature reminded me of God and reinforced in me the awe of His creation and of course, of God Himself.

This travelling eventually led me to the state of Texas. It was there in Houston that I decided to settle down and stay with a couple of friends. We rented a townhouse together and I landed a great job that paid very well. I was having the time of my life feeling grown up and responsible and free. I enjoyed my weekly conversations with my mom and loved being surprised at the monthly care packages she sent me, discovering the things she lovingly selected and packed inside. But my false sense of independence, success and security would soon be shattered.

On this particular day, a Friday, my roommates' department had to work overtime and mine didn't. Upon getting a ride and being dropped off home by a fellow co-worker, I realized that I didn't have a key to get inside. I decided since it was a beautiful day that I would walk to the nearest supermarket about two miles away and buy some steaks we could grill out for dinner. I was figuring by the time I returned, my roommates would be home. I made the quarter mile trek up the isolated street leading from our townhome community and turned right, onto the main road toward the grocery store.

After selecting and purchasing the finest cuts of sirloin I could find, I began making my way home with the bag of steaks tucked safely underneath my arm. I finally reached the road leading back to the townhouses. I hadn't walked very far down when a car pulled up beside me. I turned and saw a man waving me over to his car. As I took a few steps toward him, he asked me directions to the nearest gas station through the passenger side window. I stopped walking and held my bag of steaks tighter beneath my arm to protect them from theft as I felt a little uneasy. I then told the man I didn't know because I had recently moved to the state and wasn't very familiar with the area yet and began walking again, believing I had brushed him off. Very naive, I know that now, but not then, as I was just a small-town girl unfamiliar with what can happen in big cities.

A few moments later, the car came up beside me from the opposite direction, closer to me this time and with the car door open. The driver told me he was going to get him some white sugar. He lunged toward me and grabbed me by my lower lady private parts, trying to pull me toward him, breaking open the zipper on my pants, popping off the button, and ripping them at the seam in the process. I, completely shocked, jumped back and in doing so, somehow got out of his grip. He pounced on me again grabbing my arm this time, squeezing it so tightly it brought tears to my eyes. He began pulling me in an attempt to get me inside his car. Without even thinking, acting in sheer panic and pure natural instinct, I tried to slap him in the face with all of my strength. My aim was slightly off however, and rather than slap him, I gouged his face as my long fingernails raked across it, collecting his skin beneath them.

In that moment, he released my arm to put his hands to his face. When he pulled them back and saw blood on them, he became enraged. I took advantage of that split second, he let go of my arm, and began to run toward the townhome model in the field behind me, on the right side of the road. I heard him yelling, calling me vile names, and heard the twisted things he promised he was going to do to me, spewing the most vulgar language and speaking of the most lewd acts.

At that moment, another car turned onto the road and the man sped away. By this time, I had reached the curved brick sign in front of the townhouse model, advertising the new townhome community. I slunk down and sat with my back to the sign, hidden by the tall weeds. My heart was pounding fast and furiously as it hit home that he had intended to rape me.

I sat trembling in terror for the longest time. Once my breathing had slowed and I was able to catch my breath, I decided it was time to get back home. As I was standing up, I heard a car driving down the road and was gripped with fear once again and dropped back down because the road leading back to the townhomes had scarce traffic as there was no outlet. The only traffic on it was either to the new apartment complex to the left or to the new townhomes to the right, at the road's end. Every time I heard a car, I was sure it was him. Again, I waited until it was quiet, and attempted to get up to go home. But again, I heard a car at that moment. This happened several more times. I don't know for how long because I had lost all sense of time, but it was now dusk.

I determined the only way I was going to make it back was by not getting up again, but rather by crawling. I laid flat on my belly, bag of steaks in my right hand, and slowly began to crawl, dragging myself across the weedy, sandy, and gravely ground. I moved just a little and would stop as I didn't want the wiggling weeds to draw attention to me and give up my position. Night had now fallen, and darkness surrounded me. I decided I would get up and try to make it back. As soon as I got up on my hands and knees though, I saw headlights piercing the darkness and was overtaken by paralyzing fright again and dropped back down flat on the ground.

I would continue to crawl on my tummy, a little at a time, stop, and then crawl a little more for what seemed like an eternity. Once again, I decided to get up and make a run for it, but once again, as I began, there were headlights on the road. Back down I went as my heart raced and pounded within my chest. I silently cried out for God to help me as it felt as though my lower abdomen was rubbed raw and I wasn't sure how much longer I could do this. I got up on my hands and knees again and could see faint light up ahead. I knew I was close to the road that would lead me home. I stood up to make a run for it. Upon standing, I realized I only had about 30 yards to go to make it.

I started to run for my life but as soon as I got to the end of the field beside the road where I would turn right and head home, headlights popped on, blinding me. And out of the darkness, I heard that evil voice yell out, "Aha! I've got you now!" followed by a string of degrading curses. I couldn't believe it! I didn't even think about it, but out of desperation, just screamed at the top of my lungs, "Why can't you just leave me alone and go away?"

Right then, I heard a dog start barking, saw a porch light turn on across the street, and heard a voice yelling, asking what was going on and then inquiring if I was all right. Upon seeing the light and hearing the dog, the car sped away squawking its tires. I looked over and saw a little old lady on her front porch with her little dog barking like crazy beside her. I shouted out a grateful thank you as I raced home. I didn't mean to be rude, but I didn't want to stop and chat in case that man came back for me.

My roommates had been worried sick and had been driving around trying to find me earlier. They were jubilant to see me until they realized I was a hot mess. I had a large black bruise on my arm in the shape of a palm, fingers, and a thumb. The undersides of my forearms were all scratched up. My hair was covered with weeds and seeds and my pants were undone due to the broken zipper and missing button. My underwear could be seen because of the ripped seam. Above the waistband of my panties, my stomach was scratched, red and raw with embedded dirt and small gravel from dragging myself across the field. Upon hearing what had happened, they called the police, who recommended I didn't change or clean up until after they came to see me and made a report.

When the police arrived, one officer sat down on the couch next to me and the other sat in the recliner across from me. As they began interviewing me, they were asking me to be specific. It was very difficult for me to relive the whole thing and relay it to them but got worse when they made me say every crude word that was spoken to me. Then they told me that my statement "I was grabbed between the legs" wasn't good enough for the report, as that could be anywhere from my ankles, to my knees, to my thighs. They told me I had to be very specific and made me say the name of my body part that was grabbed, and it felt as though I was being violated all over again.

When the interview was finally over, the detectives told me that I was very lucky I only had a sexual assault and attempted rape because there had been three actual rapes within a five-mile radius within the last week. They informed me that all of the descriptions of the man and vehicle matched what I had described. They assured me they were going to catch this serial rapist promising that they would hunt him down like an animal just as he did to me. They said they would be in touch, keeping me informed of the case. I didn't feel better at all by their words, but I did thank God that I got away without being raped.

A few days later, I got a call from the detective in charge of the case informing me that they got him and thanks to my scratching his face, there was no doubt he was the perpetrator. They then informed me that the three girls who had been raped were reluctant to testify, but if I would, they would agree to. I didn't want to, but I did want to help those other girls, so I consented. After that, things went from bad to worse when a new detective was assigned to the case. Although he had the report, he wanted to hear what happened himself and made me retell the whole thing. And once more, it felt as though I was violated all over again.

Just as I was beginning to get a little bit more back to normal with the nightmares occurring less frequently, I got a call from the police department again. The lead detective went on vacation and a new detective was assigned as lead on the case and wanted to interview me to hear what happened in my own words. And as before, I felt violated again as he made me repeat every foul thing. I couldn't take it any longer. It felt as though every time I had to discuss what had happened, a wound was ripped open again and healing couldn't take place. I called to talk to my mom once again and she begged me to come home once more. This time I didn't care about the successful career I would be leaving behind or the accomplishments I had made for myself in life, and so I did. I went home.

I had no idea that God was working on my behalf behind the scenes, or that He had good plans for my life. I didn't know He intended to take what the enemy had meant for evil and turn it around for my good. But He was. He had a plan for my life before He set the foundation of the earth and unbeknownst to me, He was bringing it to fruition. He was working all things out. I didn't know what my future held, but He did. Although I wasn't walking as close to Him as I had before, although I wasn't praying and reading my Bible on a regular basis, although I wasn't
seeking His will in what I did in my life or attending church, He was still faithful. He hadn't left nor forsaken me; He hadn't forgotten me.

Thank you, Father, for being faithful to me and not forgetting me as you promise in your Word. Isaiah 49:15-16 "…I will not forget you. See, I have inscribed you on the palms of My hands" Joshua 1:5 "…I will not leave you nor forsake you…"

I was forgiven and not forgotten. Not that I deserved it, but because God is true to His Word. Second Thessalonians 3:3 "But the Lord is faithful, who will establish you and guard you from the evil one." Second Timothy 2:13, "If we are faithless, He remains faithful; He cannot deny Himself."

I'm aware some of you may be wondering how in the world I could think God was working for good on my behalf after that, and how I can consider being saved from the evil one after my attack. I understand, but I did escape with only a sexual assault and attempted rape rather than actually being raped and that was the least of it. Read on and just see what good He worked for me!

CHAPTER FOUR
GOD'S GUIDING HAND

I was back home at last! It was so comforting seeing Mom and the rest of my family again. Being home was a huge step forward in my healing process. My nights were no longer tormented with the nightmares of reliving my attack over and over again. They had finally ceased, and life was slowly but surely returning to normal for me. I had, however, lost contact with my friends while I was away. But I was content to just hang out with my sister and baby niece, my brother, and my mom.

After a couple of weeks being home, I went with my mom one Saturday for lunch at a bar and grill uptown. While we were sitting at our table, a guy came up to me and asked, "Hey Terra, do you remember me?" After looking at him a little closer, I realized I did know him. We weren't friends by any means, but we had a couple of classes together back in high school. I mostly remembered him shooting spit wads at me through a straw while in geometry class. Anyway, he told me he lived in the apartment upstairs, and was having a get together later that evening about eight o'clock and that I should come.

My mom agreed that I should go. She thought I would enjoy myself getting out and socializing rather than just sitting at home by myself watching television or listening to the stereo because she was going out with some friends later. She offered to give me a ride there if I wanted. I considered it for a moment, and then I told Jimmy I would be there at seven o'clock to help him get ready for it also. He agreed and said he would give me a ride home after.

Mom dropped me off promptly at seven o'clock. When Jimmy answered the door and invited me in, I could see he definitely needed some help as his apartment was easily identifiable as a bachelor's pad. After wiping down his counter tops and dining room table, getting out some bowls and filling them with pretzels, peanuts, potato and corn chips, I set the bowls around the apartment, and then quickly ran his vacuum over his carpeting in the living room. Jimmy and I then sat down at the dining table and started talking as the stereo played in the background. He began asking me if I remembered certain people then proceeded to fill me in on what was going on in their lives.

While sitting across from Jimmy, I heard a knock on his door and looked past him as it opened. There, standing in the doorway, I saw the most gorgeous man I had ever seen in my life. He had dark curly hair, a dark moustache and green eyes. All sounds ceased. I couldn't hear the stereo anymore nor could I hear Jimmy talking to me any longer although I could still see his mouth moving. In that split second, I heard a voice in my right ear say, "That is the man you're going to marry." Then I saw a rather ugly girl appear at his side, her arm on his. I shook my head to clear it because I noted he was taken, and all sound returned.

At this point, people were arriving in droves. Many of them remembered me from high school and came over to say hi. I eventually moved to the living room and talked with some others I remembered and others still from my old neighborhood. After talking to a guy I had tutored in ninth grade civics class for a while, I excused myself and got up to use the restroom. When finished, I went and sat back at the table as Jimmy had motioned me over. He introduced me to some people I didn't know, and we all sat around talking as the night went on.

Out of the corner of my right eye, I noticed someone sit down in the empty chair next to me. When I looked over, I saw it was that gorgeous guy I had spotted before. When I turned toward him, he said, "Hi!" I asked him where his girlfriend was and he set me straight, letting me know she wasn't his girlfriend, just a girl he knew that had asked him for a ride.

He then asked me my name and started the conversation going. He told me his name was Bill and started asking me questions about my life. I was more than happy to oblige him with the basics, starting with where I had graduated high school from through to just getting home from Texas a short while ago. I only shared the things I felt safe and comfortable discussing. After talking for a couple of hours, Bill asked me if I needed a ride home. I explained to him that Jimmy was going to bring me home afterward but thanked him for the offer.

A couple of weeks later, Sherri, a girl I had met at Jimmy's house, invited me over to her and her husband Robbie's place, explaining they were having a few friends over for pizza and to play cards Friday night. I accepted and looked forward to the coming weekend. A short while after arriving at Sherri and Robbie's, Bill walked in. As it turned out, Robbie and Bill were good buddies. Seeing Bill again made my heart flutter and took my breath away. I wasn't sure I liked it. He eventually made his way over to me and asked me if I wanted to go bowling next weekend with him and a group of his friends, adding that Sherri and Robbie were going as well.

It was then I explained to him I didn't want to be in a relationship with anyone, as I had gone through a horrific incident in Texas and just needed to sort my life out. I added I just thought he should know, but if he wanted to get together sometimes, to just go out and have some fun, I was okay with that. He assured me this was just a group of friends getting together to go bowling. I consented and gave Bill my phone number when he asked for it. When Friday night arrived, I went bowling and had a really enjoyable time with everyone.

Saturday afternoon Bill called me, and we talked for a while. Sunday afternoon he called again, and we just talked, not about anything in particular, we just shot the breeze. As a matter of fact, Bill called me almost every day for the next three weeks and I was beginning to look forward to his calls. During one of our conversations, he asked me if I wanted to go bowling with him this upcoming Saturday night and I agreed. When Bill arrived to pick me up, I introduced him to my mom and then we were off to the bowling alley.

When we arrived, the leagues were still bowling, so we had to wait for teams to finish before the open bowling could begin. Bill led me over to a table to wait and pulled out a chair for me to sit in. He went up and added his name to the open bowling wait list and returned to the table with two bottles of pop. As we were talking, the overhead loudspeaker interrupted as it blared out, Open bowling reservation for Kern. Bill said to me, his twinkling hazel eyes the color of honey this night, "Come on, baby, that's for us."

It hit me like a ton of bricks. "What? Bill is Bill Kern? Oh, my Lord, no!" my brain screamed. You see, I had gone to the same high school as Bill and although I didn't know him very well, I knew of him. He had a bad reputation as a huge troublemaker, a bad boy, and most certainly not the kind of guy I would ever associate with. I'm going to be open and transparent with you here. I'm not proud of this at all, it's just where I was at. The first thing I did was look all around the bowling alley to see if there was anyone I knew there, who would see me with him. Shallow, I know.

But then, I calmed myself down, thinking, "Hey, you've

changed since high school and obviously, so has he. You've done some growing up and he has too. He is so kind, caring and such a gentleman. He does have a good heart. He drops everything to help a friend or family member in need. You do like him, that's why you're here with him. Give this a chance and see where it goes. I mean, you didn't even recognize him when you met him at Jimmy's."

I have to again marvel at God's wisdom and at His sense of humor too. As He was guiding my path toward His purpose for me and my life, He preordained that I wouldn't learn of Bill's true identity until I was invested. I had just introduced him to my mom after all. God knew that if I had known that Bill was Bill Kern from high school, I would not have given him the time of day. It would have been all over before it even began. I hadn't cared to know Bill's last name before, because I wasn't interested in a serious relationship and it just didn't matter to me.

Apparently, God had other plans for me as from that point forward, Bill and I were inseparable and on the one-year anniversary from our first date, Bill proposed to me and I accepted. I had later asked him if he knew who I was when we met at Jimmy's and he said that he did. I asked him why he didn't say anything then, and he just looked at me as if he were saying, really? Then he asked me, "Why do you think?" I just laughed because I knew he was right. Anyway, I am so thankful God was guiding me by His hand, for in several months down the road, the greatest tragedy I have ever experienced would occur. And if it weren't for Bill, I don't know if I would have made it through…

I unexpectedly awoke sitting straight up in bed. I felt something, but of what, I wasn't sure. It's hard to put into words, but it felt as though something had been cut off from my soul, like I was an astronaut and the line keeping me from drifting away in space, away from my spacecraft, had been severed. I looked over at the clock and saw the time as 6:25 in the morning and laid back down to go to sleep as we had all been out late at a family wedding reception.

Approximately a half hour later, I was awoken again by a persistent pounding on the front door. I groggily made my way upstairs and answered it to find two police officers at the door. They informed me my mom had been in a car accident, that she was at the hospital, and I needed to go up there and sign some papers for her care. I immediately began to panic and asked if she was okay. The police officers calmed me down by telling me she had only suffered some scrapes, bumps and bruises, but needed me there as soon as possible. I got Bill and my brother up, explained everything, and we were soon out the door, Bill driving us to the hospital.

On the way, I was wondering why I needed to sign papers for Mom if she only had bumps and bruises. It wasn't making sense to me at all! But when we came upon her car smashed on the highway and saw some of her possessions still scattered about, I realized it was a horrific scene and I knew Mom had to be badly hurt. Bill understood that too and started speeding.

Upon entering the hospital, I was ushered into a small room while Bill and my brother waited outside. A woman handed me some of my mom's belongings, stating they had been doing everything they could to help her, but she wasn't responding. I didn't realize it at the time, but she was telling me my mom had died. I would later learn the accident occurred at 6:25 that morning and that she was dead on scene when help arrived, but they were able to revive her in the ambulance, however, lost her again at the hospital. The lady then asked me to fill out some paperwork while I waited as they prepared for us to see her. I went and sat with my brother and Bill and began filling out the consent forms.

Suddenly, a gurney went rushing by with my mom on it. We were told that her spleen had been severely damaged, but they successfully repaired it, stopped the bleeding, and were now taking her to a different hospital by ambulance. They told us to meet her there. We rushed to the car and followed. Once there, my brother started making phone calls to the rest of the family. We were advised that when my sister arrived, we would get a briefing on Mom's condition.

When my sister got to the hospital, we were again taken into a private room and were told Mom's injuries were extensive and she had clinically died several times, but they were able to revive her. We were told she had many internal injuries and her prognosis wasn't good. They further informed us that if she wasn't so young, they wouldn't even have tried to save her at all. I immediately began praying for her.

As some of our small family began to arrive, we were shown to a waiting room in ICU. Concern was written all over everyone's faces as we waited for an update. Finally, a nurse came in. She let us know that miraculously, Mom was no longer unconscious. She shared with us she had talked to Mom and Mom didn't remember the car accident, and even more miraculous, Mom didn't feel any pain. The nurse further explained that Mom couldn't talk because her trachea was crushed, she couldn't hear out of one ear because her eardrum was shattered, but she could squeeze our hand and answer yes or no with her head. She told us we would have to speak loudly so Mom could hear us when it was our turn, and only two at a time would be allowed in, but we couldn't stay for more than ten minutes.

I was allowed to go in first and my dad said he wanted to go with me. I agreed. When I saw Mom, I was hit with the reality that she really was in bad shape as I saw all of the equipment hooked up to her and how swollen and black and blue, she was. My dad squeezed my hand for support as I stepped up to her and spoke loudly. Mom squeezed my hand and slightly nodded or shook her head as I talked with her. I was getting really choked up and didn't want her to hear it in my voice, so I told her that I was praying for her. At that, she nodded her head vigorously. Next my dad spoke to her. I don't recall what he said except when he told her he would take care of the kids. Again, there was a vigorous nod and then Mom lost consciousness again.

As the members of our small family arrived, Mom would regain consciousness again so that every single one of us was able to go in and speak to her. It was the most agonizing couple of days of my life, and after thirty-nine and a half hours after the accident, Mom succumbed to her injuries and we lost her. I couldn't believe she was gone.

I was completely devastated. I spiraled into deep depression as I grieved her. I never realized everybody has their own unique scent until I stepped inside the house after Mom was gone and I smelled her there. I didn't want to stay at home with my little brother and his best friend who had moved in with us, because it was too painful. My dad insisted I come and stay with him and my stepmom, but I didn't want to. Bill's mom graciously allowed me to stay at her house with Bill, and I accepted. I don't know how I made it through with my brother and sister arranging for her service, or even through her memorial. It is all a blur to me still to this day.

I didn't want to do anything except be by Bill. My friends would call and invite me to go shopping or go to the beach, my favorite things to do, but I declined. I couldn't eat anything and cried all of the time. Bill's mom tried to get me to eat but I just couldn't. For three weeks I lived on nothing but coffee and cigarettes. I dropped twenty-eight pounds in those weeks and appeared very skeletal. My dad and stepmom and others were worried that I was going to literally starve myself to death and die of a broken heart.

Then one morning, Bill and his mom sat me down at the table with a yogurt and a sliced orange in front of me. They were coaxing me to eat. I got down one slice of orange and one bite of yogurt and just couldn't eat any more. Bill's mom then spoke to me. She said, "Terra, imagine your mom up in heaven looking down on you. Do you think she's saying, 'That's right, Terra, continue to starve yourself to death so you can come and join me because I miss you dearly and want you here with me?' Or do you think she's saying, 'Terra, you need to eat, honey, so that you can live and get married and have children so that I can live on through you and your children and your children's children?'"

I don't know how to explain this, but it was like I actually heard both my mom and God speaking to me. I knew right then and there I needed to eat and snap out of this downward spiral I was in. I told Bill's mom she was right and finished the yogurt and orange. I told her I did want to get married and start living my life. I explained to her that I didn't even know how to begin to plan a wedding though. She said that wouldn't be a problem, she would help Bill and me. And that is exactly what she did. The preparation is kind of a blur to me. But with Bill's mom, and my dad and stepmom, whom I had long since forgiven for everything, working together, Bill and I were married a month and a half later.

I am so thankful for God's hand guiding my life behind the scenes. The attack in Texas brought me home at just the right time to meet the man who would become my husband, and to have me home when my mom would pass away, with the love of my life by my side, to guide me through the deep sorrow. If I had not come home from Texas when I did, I never would have met Bill as we most certainly didn't run in the same circles. If I had recognized him from school, I wouldn't have given him one iota of my time. If I had still been in Texas when my mom was killed, I honestly don't think I would have forgiven myself. I only had her for a few short years before she was gone and for a year of that, I was away.

You see, God divinely guides the footsteps of those He has called according to His purpose. Some refer to it as the providence of God which is simply God knowing your future and making arrangements and preparations for when you reach certain points along your path in life. He makes sure when you get to those points, you get what He has meant for you so you can begin walking in your destiny. Even when we make some wrong choices, He will begin to tweak, correct, and adjust things to get us back on track again because of His unfailing love for us. We can find God's guiding hand all throughout His Word.

If Moses had not been kicked out of the palace of Egypt and become a sheep herder, he would never have been able to lead his people out of their bondage. If Daniel had not been captured, he would never have been the second most powerful man in Babylon for three consecutive kings' reigns. If David's father had not sent him to his brothers at that precise time, he would have never slain Goliath and later become king. If there wasn't a census decreed, Mary and Joseph would not have been where prophecy said Jesus would be born. And the list goes on and on.

Romans 8:28 "And we know that all things work together for good to those who love God, to those who are the called according to His purpose."

Hallelujah! I give God praise! And I join Joseph, who was sold into slavery by his very own brothers, in saying, "But as for you, you meant evil against me; but God meant it for good, in order to bring it about as it is this day…" Genesis 50:20

The providence of God continues throughout all our lives and will do so until God's plan for earth is complete. I like to lovingly refer to God's providence or His guiding hand as the most supreme GPS system, or in other words, our heavenly global positioning system. God knows we are at point A and knows we need to get to point B. But if we veer to the left, right, or take the wrong fork in the road, if we miss where we should have turned due to our distracted driving, He just states, "No problem, I got this…recalculating!"

As you can probably guess, God's loving, guiding hand didn't stop there in my life as He was guiding me on to what would by my destiny. Read on to see the marvelous, wondrous things He brought for both Bill and me.

CHAPTER FIVE
FROM DESPAIR TO DESTINY

Once Bill and I were married, I began to lean on him more and more and rely on God less and less. I felt as though I was in a place where I had someone who truly loved me, all of me, for the first time in my life. It felt as though Bill had seen into my heart and after seeing both the wheat and the chaff, still loved me. At the same time, my relationship with my dad was somewhat strained as he told me after my marriage that he only gave it six months. He clearly believed Bill was not the one for me and our marriage would fail. Because of that, I distanced myself from him.

Wherever Bill led, I followed. Our weekends were spent partying with his friends, and I slowly but surely left God behind and incorporated the ways of the world into my life, giving way a little here and a little there. I wasn't praying, reading my Bible, going to church, or considering His ways any longer. I relied on Bill for everything.

It wasn't long into my pregnancy with our first child that Bill began to desert me and chose to go out with his buddies partying rather than stay home with me. This hurt me deeply and when I tried to talk to him about how I felt, he would get angry and arguments ensued. I felt as though he no longer loved me. I was devastated and began to call my dad and talk to him again, allowing our once strained relationship to build and strengthen.

I was, however, eagerly awaiting the birth of our child believing things would change once the baby arrived. But I was sadly mistaken. Bill began drinking even more after the birth of our daughter. It was no longer just on the weekends but began to happen during the week as well. It got to the point where his routine was to come home from work, shower and change his clothes, eat the dinner I had prepared for him, and then leave to go out drinking with his buddies, leaving me and our new daughter all alone night after night. He wouldn't come home until late and when he did arrive, I was right there to protest his unacceptable behavior, leading to more heated arguments. So much for my hopes of him growing up, acting responsible, and giving up alcohol once he became a father.

I was completely distraught, heartbroken, and in deep despair. My dad was livid and wanted me and his new little granddaughter out of the entire mess. He came up with what he believed was the perfect solution. And that solution put me and my new little family on the road to our destiny.

One day while Bill was at work, my dad stopped over and told me he had a gift for me. He presented me with divorce papers he had his attorney draw up. My dad explained all I had to do was sign them and then Bill would be legally served which would end all of my torment. I was flabbergasted and shocked. I informed my dad that I wasn't sure if that is what I wanted. He left the papers with me and told me to think about it. And think about it, I did. Actually, I couldn't get away from thinking about it and it was torturous.

I believed getting a divorce was a sin and I didn't want to sin against God. In addition, Bill and I, while discussing marriage, had made a vow to one another that if we were married, divorce was not an option. With both of us coming from broken homes, we knew divorce was not healthy for children or adults either, for that matter.

There were other sinful things I had participated in that hadn't seemed to bother me at all. But I couldn't escape the thoughts of divorce being a sin, and vowing divorce wasn't an option. On the other hand, I also battled with not wanting my little baby growing up with an alcoholic father. I had some childhood friends whose fathers were alcoholics and that wasn't pretty or healthy either. This battle took place in my mind for days and brought me to my fateful night.

I was lying in my bed, unable to sleep because I was bawling my eyes out over Bill being out drinking with the boys once again. My body was so wracked with forlorn sobs, it was tough to catch my breath. In an attempt to calm myself down, I swiped my swollen and stinging eyes with the back of my hand, brushing away the salty tears so I could see. I turned my head, looked over at the clock, and saw it glowing the time as 2 o'clock in the morning. My heart felt as though it were breaking in two. I was at my wits end. This is not the marriage I had anticipated or the way I wanted my two-month-old daughter to be raised.

I took in another deep breath and as I let it out, I began to cry out to God. As I prayed, all of the troubles of my heart began to pour out. The floodgates had been opened, the dam compromised, and everything came rushing out.

"Dear God, please help me. Bill's out drinking again, and I can't take it anymore! I don't know what to do. The divorce papers Daddy had drawn up by his attorney are just waiting for my signature. I don't want to sign them. I don't want to sin against you, but I don't want to live with an alcoholic for a husband and I don't want the precious baby girl you gave me to grow up with a father addicted to alcohol either. I thought his drinking was a young man thing and when he became a father, he would grow up, give it up, and become a responsible man. That hasn't happened.

I have made such a mess of my life and worse yet, I now have a new little life that I am responsible for too. Please come and live within me again and lead me in the way to go. Speak to me again, Lord. I tried living my life on my own and have made a huge catastrophe of it. I need you in my life again. Lead me and guide me in the way to go by your Holy Spirit, I pray."

Suddenly, I felt as light as a feather, as though I were levitating. I was sure when I opened my eyes I would be a mere few inches from the ceiling. But when I opened them, I was still lying in my bed and not floating at all. I felt a peaceful calm come over me as I looked to my right and saw a faint light in the shape of a long robe with outstretched arms and distinct hands reaching out to me. I heard a voice in the room audibly and gently say to me, "Fear not my little child, for I will take care of things."

The next thing I knew, I was awoken by the sound of Bill stumbling through the house and falling onto the couch in the living room. He had grown smart and knew better to come into the bedroom lest he wake me and my wrath. But this time, I found myself thanking God that Bill had made it home safely and rolled over to go back to sleep. This was a new thing for me. You see, already a change had taken place within my heart because I normally would have whipped out of bed and tore into him, yapping and nipping like a high strung poodle; letting him know exactly what I thought of him and his drinking. But not this time, for I was encompassed by a sweet peace. It was impossible to have been in God's very presence and to remain the same and unchanged.

Sunday rolled around and my dad and stepmom stopped by on their way to church again and asked if I wanted to go. I literally felt something inside of me leap for joy! And for the first time, I told them I wanted to go rather than making my tired and worn out excuses.

Every Sunday they invited me, and I went. Every Sunday I invited Bill and he declined. Every Sunday God was moving in the church and testimonies were shared on the astonishing things God had blessed people with in their lives. Every Sunday, Pastor prayed for people and the Holy Spirit moved. And every Sunday, I came home and shared these things with Bill.

One Sunday shortly thereafter, I was in the living room dressed for church, holding our sweet baby girl wearing her new velvet and lace dress, when out of the blue, Bill walked into the living room dressed in his best clothes. He informed me he wanted to go to church and see about the things I had been telling him about God. I was so surprised and even more happy!

After the sermon, Pastor instructed the organist to play as he prayed. He silently bowed his head and after a few moments, made an announcement. He shared with the congregation that there was someone whom God was calling and asked everyone to bow their heads, close their eyes, and pray silently. Pastor invited whomever God was speaking to, to come forward. There was nothing but organ music quietly playing, but no movement.

I knew God was calling Bill, so I gently reached over and touched his hand. I lovingly whispered if he wanted me to go up with him, I would. He promptly slung my hand back on my lap whispering sharply back to me, "If I'm going up there it will be because I want to, not because you or anyone else wants me to."

I was shocked and hurt but continued to pray as my faith-filled heart pounded within my chest. The church was silent except for the organist playing. I could barely hear that divine music over the sound of blood pulsing and thundering through my veins and reverberating in my ears. Pastor called for that person once more as the organ music gently floated throughout the sanctuary, and to my delight, Bill stood up, walked to the altar, and dedicated his life to God!

Our lives and marriage were transformed that day. Bill gave up alcohol on the spot. He hungered for the things of God and we were in church every time the doors were open. Bill began to serve our pastor in many capacities from hard labor, to ushering, to playing the drums during praise and worship. I began teaching Sunday school classes and organizing fun activities and games for the children at all of the special events. We were truly blessed, and our family prospered. We were soon blessed with another baby girl and life was good. God is so awesome and worthy to be praised, for the blessings didn't stop there.

In my times of prayer and studying the Bible, as well as reading books written by great men and women of God, the Holy

Spirit began to speak to me and show me wondrous things. One time after reading and prayer, He spoke to me and told me Bill was going to have John's position at work. John was Bill's boss, the manager of the quality control department. I shared this with Bill and he just looked at me and smiled. Less than two weeks later, Bill came home from work with a huge grin. He said, "You're not going to believe this! John put in his two weeks' notice as he found another job and is leaving the company. He recommended me as his replacement and the company accepted his recommendation. In two weeks, I will be the quality control manager!"

I smiled at Bill and just said, "I believe it! Congratulations honey!" This truly was a blessing and cause to celebrate as it came with a much-needed pay raise because our little family had grown. God is so good!

Another time after reading my Bible, I heard the Spirit of the Lord say to me that He was calling Bill and me into ministry. I instantly countered with, "But I don't want to be a 'church lady!'" I heard Him laugh and respond back, telling me He didn't want me to be a "church lady" but wanted me to be me, wanted me to be exactly who He created me to be. I pondered upon this and kept it quietly tucked away in my heart.

Allow me to explain my above response to God. Up until this point, almost all of the women in ministry I had known in the churches I had grown up in were to me, frumpy and grumpy. What I mean by that is they all wore drab clothing lacking vibrant color or style. They were all very stern and were always scolding, reprimanding and chastising while waving that pointer finger. They were quick to point out unacceptable behavior and slow to smile, compliment or praise. There was no fun or laughter to be found in them at all and that was the complete opposite of who I was. This was my perception of women in ministry and as I'm sure you've heard before; one's perception is one's reality. But God had plans to change that.

It wasn't long before God began to make our church nest very uncomfortable. Little did we know that He had determined it was time for us to start learning to spread our wings and fly. As it states in Deuteronomy 32:11 "As an eagle stirs up its nest…" meaning to make it uncomfortable, God did with us. To better understand this concept, we need to know how an eagle assembles its nest. The eagle starts with thorns as a strong outer shell of protection and then adds twigs to form another layer, then an additional layer of thorns to withstand any enemy or predator's penetration. Next comes another layer of twigs, and then on top of that, the eagle builds a layer of grass to create what we would think of as perhaps a cushion on a couch or a mattress in a crib. But the eagle doesn't stop there. The last step of the mother eagle's nest building is the plucking of her very own feathers to lay down the soft, snug and comfortable layer for the baby eaglets. Here the eaglets are cared for, nurtured, loved and fed until they grow to a certain age.

The next phase of training eaglets is to slowly dismantle the nest, removing the soft down first, then the cushion of grass and lastly, rearranging the twigs with the spiky ends up to make it extremely uncomfortable for them to encourage them to leave. The eagle is preparing to teach them to fly and that is where we found ourselves. We left that nest and it felt as though we were in a freefall. Again, just as in Deuteronomy 32:11 "…that spreads its wings to catch them…" Before we hit the bottom, God caught us and flew us to our next destination just as the mother eagle catches her eaglets safely and furthers their ongoing preparation.

Father God sent us to a different church for more instruction. My stepmom, whom I had grown close with, recommended it to us. Here we were taught to recognize our unique gifts and the call the Lord had given us and be trained in and to begin to exercise them. We were again blessed with another child, our third, while serving. This time we were blessed with a son who was an answer to prayer and literally, a miracle birth. Details will be given in a later chapter.

Once we had gleaned the training God had for us there, again we were pushed out of the uncomfortable nest and delivered to the church where we received further training and our call to the ministry was set in motion. We were ordained as ministers and we began serving on the ministerial staff. We had learned to not only fly, but to soar to great heights in the things of God. Of course, this is a brief synopsis of our training, but glory to Father God in the highest as He has good plans for all of His children.

CHAPTER SIX
HE WILL GIVE HIS ANGELS CHARGE OVER YOU

In this chapter, I am going to share the times God sent one of His angels to keep me safe in a variety of different ways throughout my life as He has asked of me. We will then delve into scripture and see what God tells us about His angels in the following chapter. We'll discover what angels do and what they do not do so that we are not deceived or believe an angelic encounter to be "woo woo" or "spooky spiritual", leading to putting too much emphasis on them and in turn, allowing us to be led astray.

My first encounter with an angel came when I was just a tiny little girl. I was very excited as my mom's best friend Sunny was going to take my brother and me up north to visit her mother. I was a small child and don't remember what town or which great lake in Michigan we were going to. But I was thrilled Sunny was bringing her niece and nephew up as well, so we would have playmates around our own age.

The morning after we arrived at Sunny's mom's house, we began packing up to go to the beach. We were going to spend the day there at the lake and have a picnic as well. Sunny told me I would be able to collect driftwood along the beach. I was delighted to hear that because my mom used driftwood in some of the crafts she created as a hobby and I wanted to get her some.

After the car was parked, we all had our arms loaded up with the things we would be using that day and headed down toward the beach. Off to one side of the beach, Sunny chose a secluded area away from the rest of the crowd and near an inlet where reeds grew near the shore's edge. She laid out a couple of blankets for us to sit on and instructed us to put all of our other things needed for the beach on them too. Our spot was under a huge tree that had a big fat branch low enough that we could climb up and sit on it, but not so low as to bump our heads on it when we sat on the blankets.

The first thing we did after setting up our spot was head midway down the beach toward the shore to the cement changing rooms there. The building was made of concrete and was circular and you had to go halfway around before the changing rooms appeared. Once we had changed into our swimsuits, we returned to our spot, packed our regular clothes away and grabbed our towels, blow up water toys, as well as our pails and shovels, and headed back to the shore. After we had played for a while, Sunny rounded us up to head back to eat lunch.

Spread over one of the blankets was a red-and-white plaid tablecloth and plates for us all. After I had finished my fried chicken, potato salad, chips and pickle, I headed toward the inlet to look for driftwood for my mom. After collecting a few pieces, I heard Sunny calling me back frantically. She was hurriedly packing everything back up to leave. She was calling for me to come back telling me we needed to get back to the car quickly!

When I looked up, I saw the sky over the lake had turned very dark. Lightning was flashing through the blackened sky through the mounting sinister appearing clouds and the waves were large and white capped. The wind churned waters looked angry. When I saw this scene before me, I suddenly remembered a dream I had with that exact same scene. In the dream there was a bright white figure speaking to me, so bright, I couldn't make out any specific features.

As I heard the voice from the dream, I did exactly what it instructed me to do. It was like a movie running before my eyes as it came back to my remembrance. "Do not go back. Run to the changing structure on the beach." So rather than run back to Sunny and our picnic spot, I took off running toward the concrete structure in the middle of the sandy beach, in the very direction the storm was rolling in from. Sunny kept calling for me to come back and when I didn't, she dropped everything, grabbed the other children and told them to hold hands and not to let go. They all began running toward me to catch me.

Once I made it to the beach, the wind had kicked up in ferocity and the sand from the beach was stinging as the wind drove it into my bare skin. It felt as though I was being pricked by hundreds of little tiny needles. I was concentrating on the voice. "I know the sand will hurt you, but do not turn back. Keep going on toward the structure." All the people were running from the beach toward the parking lot amid screams and yelling, the complete opposite direction I was headed in. Suddenly, I could no longer hear Sunny's voice because the roar of the winds, booming of the thunder, and crashing of the waves had drowned out all other sounds other than the voice. "When you get inside, get down and stay there. Do not move, stay down."

By the time I reached the entrance to the changing house, Sunny had caught up to me with my little brother and her niece and nephew in tow. We all ran inside. I immediately dropped down against the wall, following the instructions of the voice. I heard Sunny telling the other kids to do the same. The wind howled, rain poured down from the skies, and the winds blew so hard, it sounded like they were at times howling and others, whistling. It seemed like an eternity before everything calmed down and eventually stopped.

When Sunny determined it was safe for us to emerge, we all came out and couldn't believe the sight before us. People's belongings were scattered everywhere about. Some trees were down and some of the light posts in the parking area were down also. That big old branch we had enjoyed climbing up and sitting on had cracked and fallen down right on our spot, over our belongings. If we had been there when it had fallen, we could have been seriously injured or even killed! I don't know if there had been a tornado or strong straight-line winds or even just a nasty thunderstorm, for as I stated earlier, I was very young. Nonetheless, praise be to God for the angel sent to instruct me in a dream!

The second encounter with an angel happened much later in my life after I was a grown woman, married, and had three children. Saturday had rolled around and as was routine, I took my two daughters shopping at a local department store. When we left to go shopping, it was a bit chilly as it was fall, but the sun was shining brightly and took the nip right out of the air. It was a beautiful day and my daughters and I were looking forward to our shopping excursion.

When we finally had selected the items we wanted, went through the checkouts and exited the store, we found clouds had moved in and noticed a drop in temperature. It looked like it was going to rain so I hurried the girls into the car, loaded our packages in the back of our minivan and we were off.

While driving down the highway, the skies turned darker and darker. It first started to sprinkle and by the time we turned on the road we needed to take home, it started pouring down rain, as if from buckets. I had the windshield wipers on high and still found it difficult to see. Driving was slow going. Then suddenly, the rain slowed back to a sprinkle, and then stopped completely. I breathed a sigh of relief.

I was completely stunned when it immediately started to snow. The girls complained from the back that they were freezing. I tuned on the heater as I realized the temperature was rapidly dropping. The snowflakes went from sparse little flakes to huge snowflakes, so many of them in fact, it was almost as hard to see as when the rain was coming down in torrents. We were driving in white out conditions. As we crossed over the freeway, I was overjoyed that we were not too far from home.

As we crested the hill and began to pick up speed, I tapped the brakes to slow down, but the van felt as though it was sliding. I began to tap the brakes repeatedly as we gained speed and my heartbeat sped up too as if to keep the pace. Oh no! The light at the bottom of the hill was red and traffic had stopped. We were not slowing down one bit. I frantically pushed the brake down and held it to the floor as we were sliding closer and closer to the stopped car in front of us. I realized the rain from earlier had frozen and was sheer ice below the accumulating snow.

"Jesus!" was all I was able to get out before the abrupt halt in motion occurred. I was thrust forward, and then stopped, suspended in midair, held only by the restraining of my seatbelt for a moment. Then I was slung backward again, slamming me into my seat once more. I turned around to see if the girls were all right. They let me know they were but that their seatbelts had hurt them. I told them I was sorry, but it was icy, we were sliding, and mommy couldn't stop the car in time to avoid hitting the car in front of us. I then explained I had to get out and see what kind of damage there was to the vehicles as well as check on the person in the car in front of us, to see if they were okay.

I then opened my car door and got out, slipping a little bit. I made my way to the front of the van taking little baby steps so as not to lose my footing and fall. When I reached the front, I couldn't believe my eyes! The minivan was about a foot away from the car in front of us. We hadn't hit it at all. I glanced toward the car in front of me and saw a man looking at me strangely through his rearview mirror, as though I was crazy. For a fraction of a split second, I saw through the thick snowfall an all-white form sitting on the trunk of the car in front of me with feet extended, resting on the front of our van's bumper.

Astonished, I made my way back inside, shut the door, and began to slowly drive as the light had turned green. My youngest daughter asked from the backseat if the car was crunched. I explained to her there was no damage but I needed her not to talk to me so I could concentrate on getting us the rest of the home safely because the roads were really slippery. I praised and thanked God under my breath the rest of the way home.

When we were parked securely in the driveway, I instructed the girls to get out and be careful as it was slick. My oldest daughter asked me if we had been in an accident. I told her we weren't, and she responded that we were, and she knew we were because she felt it and the seat belt hurt her. My youngest added that her chest hurt. I ushered them inside with our purchases under my arms, telling them we would talk about it once inside.

As I was helping the girls off with their coats, they both complained of it hurting them. I lifted up the shirts of them both and was met with bright red, diagonal angry marks across their chests from the seatbelts. I told them they had red marks, but they would be all right.

My husband, sitting on the couch and watching television with our little son, asked what had happened. I relayed the whole thing to him including the white form on the other car. We were all in agreement that God had given us driving mercies and had sent His angel there to protect us. Thank you, Lord!

A few years later, yet another encounter with an angel occurred. However, I didn't recognize it as an angelic intervention until after the incident. Allow me to explain. I was feeling ill, burning hot, weak, and still tired upon waking this particular morning. I called in to the elementary school where I was working as a paraprofessional to take the day off. After getting the children on the school bus, I didn't do much except fade in and out of sleep on the living room couch as a fever raged inside me.

Suddenly, I was awoken from a deep sleep by a loud pounding on the front door. I groggily made my way over to it. When I opened the door, I found a man there with a frantic look upon his face. He told me with urgency in his voice, that my couch was on fire. I looked at him as if he were wacky, looked over at the couch I had just been sleeping on, and then back at him, raising my eyebrows in a questioning manner. He shook his head and pointed to the south side of the house, saying not the one inside, but the one outside the house. My mind fully woke up at this point as I remembered the old couch we had sitting up against the house along with an old television set waiting to be loaded up and taken to the dump.

When this stranger dressed in jeans, a flannel shirt, and work boots recognized the look of understanding come over my face, he asked me if we had a hose to hook up to the spigot on the front of the house. I remembered that Bill had said it had sprung a leak and he tossed it and had not purchased a new one yet as summer had passed. I shook my head no and he asked me if we had some buckets. I ran and got him the only one we had, a five-gallon bucket. When I explained to him we only had the one, he instructed me to start filling up pots of water from the kitchen sink as he started filling the bucket from the front spigot.

Once I had a large pot full of water, I placed another under the faucet and proceeded to bring out the first. When I reached the side of the house, the stranger had pulled the burning couch away from the house and was pouring water on it from the bucket. The smoke was burning my eyes as he told me he had to pull the couch away from the house because it had ignited the vinyl siding on the house. He asked me to bring him a pot as well, to fill while he was using the five-gallon bucket. We had quite the assembly line going with the water, but the flames were spreading and growing larger on the house.

Just then, I heard the school bus stop in front of the driveway and turned as my three children were getting off the bus. They came running down the driveway with huge questioning eyes. I explained everything and instructed my two daughters to get some more pots and pans and start filling them from the bathtub. I told my son, the youngest, to stay back. As I returned to the side of the house with another pot of water, I saw the stranger pulling off burning vinyl from the house with his bare hands! He informed me he had to get the siding off the house so the wood beneath wouldn't ignite and burn.

Once all the flames were distinguished due to our team effort, the house itself had been spared from any damage. I went up to the stranger to thank him, but he spoke first. He explained that as he was passing by, he saw the flames coming from the couch and watched all of the traffic continuing on without anyone stopping to help, so he had to act. He added, as we walked from the side yard into the front, that he was surprised no fire trucks had arrived either as the flames were clearly visible from the road.

I asked him to let me get him some money to pay him in gratitude for his hard work. He waved his hand at me stating that wasn't necessary. I then asked him if he had a business card I could have so my husband could call him and thank him later, when he got home from work. He said that he did not. I beseeched of him to at least give me his name so I could publicly thank him by writing a letter to the editor of our local newspaper. He told me he didn't want me to do that.

At that point, I turned toward the house as I heard the screen door open and saw my daughters coming outside again after putting the pots and pans back inside. I turned back around to continue speaking to this gentleman but he was gone. I couldn't believe it! I asked my daughters if they had seen him leave. They said he was just gone.

My daughters and I looked up the driveway toward the road and didn't see him. We looked both to the right and to the left and there was no trace of him at all, just traffic moving normally along. I thought back and didn't remember even seeing a vehicle. I asked the girls if they remembered seeing one and the oldest replied she didn't and the youngest stated she might remember seeing a truck but wasn't really sure. Regardless, this helpful stranger had just vanished!

Did we once again experience an angelic visitation? I believe we did. Moreover, I realized shortly thereafter that I didn't feel sick anymore. The fever had disappeared, and I was no longer feeling tired and weak, but rather energized and strong. What a mighty God we serve!

God sent an angel to save my life once more approximately five years later. At this time, I had my own home business where I sold woman's fashions in the homes of women who invited me to present the pieces there. I was expected with this company, to wear their fashions as I presented. The new line that had just come out included snakeskin pieces and is what I had chosen for this evening's show. The top was a sleeveless snakeskin vest with a zipper that could be zipped and unzipped from the bottom or top. The matching skirt also had a zipper on the side.

I had everything packed in the car and was ready to go. In my hand, I had the directions my husband had given me to the home I was going to. The show this night was in a city I was not very familiar with and one full of one-way streets. And as Bill will tell you, "She can't drive her way out of a wet paper bag." That's highly over exaggerated of course but gets the point across that I don't do well with directions. Before I pulled out of the driveway, I prayed that God would give me driving mercies and have his angels encamped round about me to deliver and protect me and keep me safe from harm, just as I always did before driving.

I arrived at my destination without any glitches. I had a very successful evening and because of that, the show ran well past the time I had anticipated. It was late and dark as I loaded up the last of my pieces and shut the trunk lid. I was more than ready to get back home to my husband and children and set off on the return journey.

I had been driving for quite a while and hadn't found the road I was looking for to take me to the expressway. It was unusually hot and humid and sweat was dripping into my eyes. My car had no air conditioner as it was an older model. It didn't even have electric windows, so I manually unrolled the driver's side window down the rest of the way to help me cool down. As I looked around, I didn't recognize anything at all and had a sinking feeling that I had gotten myself lost. I then started looking for somewhere to stop and ask for directions to the freeway.

Up ahead, I spotted a gas station to my left, just before a traffic light, and decided to pull in. I drove my car up to the store, turned off the ignition, and opened the door. As my foot hit the pavement while starting to get out, I heard whoops and hollers and whistles. I glanced back and to my left and saw a bunch of hoodlums all around two cars hopped up with hydraulic systems.

The things they were saying to me as some of them began to walk toward me would make a sailor blush. More were in the cars making them jump up and down with the hydraulics. As I pulled my foot back in, I shut the car door and frantically rolled up the windows. I then realized I had unzipped all the zippers of my snakeskin outfit in hopes of keeping cool in the oppressive heat and humidity. I rolled my eyes at myself realizing what I must look like as I pushed all the locks down in the car, both in the front and back.

I was frightened and didn't want to look back and see what was happening. I laid my head down on the steering wheel and cried out, "Lord Jesus, help me!" I kept my head down on the steering wheel while wishing I had brought our only cell phone with me when suddenly, I heard a knocking on my side window. I squeezed my eyes shut, too afraid to look up. Again, I heard the knocking. I slowly raised my head and turned toward the driver side window to see who was there.

I saw a very dark-skinned man bent over and looking at me.

He motioned with his hand for me to unroll my window. I shook my head no at him and put my head back down on the steering wheel. Again, he knocked. I looked over at him and this time he smiled as he motioned for me to unroll my window. That smile was so bright and comforting. I immediately understood he wasn't one of them as I felt an unexplained peace settle over me. Somehow, I knew I could trust him and turned the window crank, rolling down my window just a crack. He said, "Come on out. I will escort you inside. They won't hurt you." He smiled again and I opened my car door as he stepped back.

Once I was out of the car, he held his elbow out for me to hold on to. It was then I was taken aback at his height. He had to be at least seven feet tall! I then noticed he was dressed in a tunic and slacks made of plain linen the color of burlap. I saw he had on simple tanned leather sandals that looked handmade. I thought it odd but was grateful for his assistance and protection.

When we reached the door of the gas station, he opened it for me and motioned for me to step inside. Once inside, I spotted the counter and began to walk toward it to ask for directions. On the way, I noticed the tall gentleman hadn't followed me inside. I was a little disappointed and uneasy but asked the man behind the counter how to get to the freeway. He told me I was almost there and only needed to go two more blocks and turn left. He said that road would lead me straight to the freeway and told me to take exit B to head back east.

Leaving the counter and heading back to the door, I saw the tall gentleman waiting just outside. I didn't dare look toward the pumps and just kept my eyes on that friendly stranger. When I pushed the door open, he laughed a deep hearty laugh as his arm made a sweeping motion across the gas station lot. I looked and saw all of the hoodlums racing back to their cars with looks of fright upon their faces. They all hopped in the vehicles and peeled out as they left. I looked back at the man still laughing. He then asked me where had they all gone and continued laughing. He told me I was safe now as we walked back to my car. He opened my car door for me and closed it after I was in, then waved goodbye to me.

I waved, backed my car around, and headed toward the road I had just come off to go home, still somewhat dazed at everything that had just transpired. When I pulled out of the gas station, the traffic light turned red. As I waited for the light to turn green, the man who had just helped me was running across the road in front of me. I again marveled at his height. Then he completely disappeared midstride right before my eyes! It was then I realized that stranger must have been an angel sent to protect me. I played it all over in my head during my drive home thanking and praising God for his protection the whole way back.

Once I returned home to my family, I saw the concern written all over their faces. My husband jumped up to meet me and gave me a bear hug. He asked me where I had been, if I was okay and what had happened. It was then that I relayed everything that had occurred earlier. My oldest teenage daughter, who worked at a store in the mall of that city, exclaimed that where I had described in getting lost was the worst part of the city. She explained it was where the hookers walked, drug dealers dealt, and murders took place! My heart palpitated, and goose bumps rose all over my body. Again, praises and thanksgiving to God proceeded out of my mouth as I put my hand over my heart. To God be the glory!

CHAPTER SEVEN
GOD'S ANGELS

Now, let's turn to the Holy Scriptures in reference to angels. There are just shy of 300 references to angels in the Word of God throughout the Old Testament and the New. Most of the favorite stories of the Old Testament shared down through the ages contain angels having major roles in them. There are also spectacular occurrences of angels assisting men of God, making announcements and carrying out God's will in the New Testament as well.

Sometimes the angels sent by God appear as men. When they came to Abraham, the angels appeared as men. Genesis18:1-2 "Then the Lord appeared to him by the terebinth trees of Mamre as he was sitting in the tent door in the heat of the day. So, he lifted his eyes and looked, and behold, three men were standing by him…" Then again in 18:22 "Then the men turned away from there and went toward Sodom." Also, we are instructed to not forget to entertain strangers in Hebrews 13:2 "Do not forget to entertain strangers, for by so doing some have unwittingly entertained angels."

Upon studying the many scriptures pertaining to angels, we find a myriad of things angels are part of and from those, we find four major roles that most fall under. But these four by no means cover all that God sends them for.

Angels are God's messengers. The word angel means messenger of God. We find many instances of angels delivering messages to God's people throughout his Word. God sent three angels to Abraham and Sarah to tell them that even in her old age, she would soon bear a son. He sent an angel to the discouraged Gideon with the message "The Lord is with you, you mighty man of valor." God sent an angel to Daniel in answer to a prayer. He sent an angel to Mary to let her know she was going to conceive and give birth to Jesus. An angel was sent to Joseph on more than one occasion to deliver messages to him with instructions on what to do. An angel was sent to the shepherds in the field to let them know Jesus had been born.

Angels protect God's people. Psalms 91:11 says, "For He shall give his angels charge over you, to keep you in all your ways". Psalms 34:7 says, "The angel of the Lord encamps all around those who fear Him and delivers them." God sent an angel to protect Daniel in the lion's den and the angel shut the mouths of the lions, so no harm came to him. In Exodus, God told the Israelites he was protecting them when He said He was sending an angel ahead of them to guard them along the way and bring them to the land He had promised them. In Second Kings, the prophet Elisha prayed that his servant would see the armies of angels God had protecting the city.

Angels praise and worship God as well as rejoice when a sinner repents. In the book of Isaiah, he saw the Lord sitting on a throne and heard one angel say to another, Holy, holy, holy is the Lord of Hosts; the whole earth is full of His Glory. In the Book of Revelation, we find the angels do not rest day or night saying Holy, holy, holy, Lord God Almighty, who was and is and is to come. We also see where John says he looked and heard the voice of many angels around the throne and the number of them was ten thousand times ten thousand and thousands of thousands. Luke 15:10 says, "Likewise, I say to you, there is joy in the presence of angels of God over one sinner who repents."

Angels are God's warriors and bring judgment. Just in reading through the Book of Revelation alone, we can see that God has given his angels charge to execute judgment. My favorite example is Revelation 12:7-9 "And war broke out in heaven; Michael and his angels fought with the dragon; and the dragon and his angels fought, but they did not prevail, nor was a place found for them in heaven any longer. So, the great dragon was cast out, that serpent of old, called the devil and Satan, who deceives the whole world; he was cast to earth, and his angels were cast out with him." Another example is in Second Kings. Here we find King Hezekiah had prayed to God asking Him to help him with his cruel enemies, the Assyrians. Second Kings 19:35 "And it came to pass on a certain night that the angel of the Lord went out, and killed in the camp of the Assyrians one hundred and eighty-five thousand; and when people arose early in the morning, there were the corpses – all dead."

God does employ his angels for more than the above as well. We can find when God's angel appeared to the donkey of a prophet before appearing to the prophet himself. We find an angel cooking food for another prophet. And we find an angel breaking disciples out of jail on two occasions. We discover Herod struck with a disease from an angel. We find in Genesis after the fall, God placed angels at the east of the Garden of Eden, and a flaming sword which turned every way, to guard the way to the tree of life. Upon seeing that God has incorporated angels from the beginning and will continue to until the end, we shouldn't be at all shocked that angels are still at play in God's plans for us today. Sometimes we are allowed to see them and sometimes we are not, but just because we can't see them does not mean that they are not there, as in many accounts in the Scriptures.

We must understand that God sends His angels. This is of vital importance. In every instance of angelic activity throughout the Holy Scriptures, we find God sends the angels. They are His servants and messengers. We do not hold idle conversations with angels. When they have a message for us, they deliver it to us and are with us until their mission from God is complete. Let me reiterate this. Angels do not hang around to have conversations or to chew the fat with us. We do not send angels, command angels, or have charge over them. God gives his angels charge over us. They do God's bidding, not ours. Let's look at Psalms 91:11 again. "For He shall give his angels charge over you, to keep you in all your ways". The Scripture does not say, For He shall give you charge over His angels to keep you in all your ways.

I know of an older woman who advertises she gives "angel readings". I've seen her at local events. She claims she can speak to your assigned angels and they tell her things about you and your life and then instructs what you should do according to the words of your angel. She then shares those things with you. Of course, she charges you for her service and makes her living this way. I can assure you she is not speaking to God's angels. It is contradictory to the Holy Scriptures.

Let's look at what Scripture does say regarding this. Second Corinthians 11:13-16 "For such are false apostles, deceitful workers, transforming themselves into apostles of Christ. And no wonder! For even Satan transforms himself into an angel of light. Therefore, it is no great thing if his ministers also transform themselves into ministers of righteousness, whose end will be according to their works."

It has also come to my attention that there are many more that do similar things. They even have names for the angels you can call upon to help you with just about anything. They claim they have one angel to pray to for when you're cold to come and warm you up from the top of your head to the bottom of your feet. Another named one to call upon for healing your pet when it is sick, another to teach you how to do magic, another to give you creative ideas even for a new hairstyle design. Apparently, there is quite a list with many of them being female.

All of this is contrary to God's word. There are no examples in Scripture of anyone praying to an angel or asking angels for help, period! We are to pray to God. We call on Him when we are in need or are in precarious situations and need divine intervention and He responds to our prayer in the way He knows is best. However, at times, His best may not include angels at all. Throughout the Word, angels always appear as male in the Bible. Only two are named, the archangel Michael and Gabriel.

Angels always praise and bless God and do God's bidding, not ours. Psalms 103:20 "Bless the Lord, you His angels, who excel in strength, who do His word, heeding the voice of His word." Psalm 148:2 "Praise Him all His angels; praise Him all His hosts!"

Do not be deceived! First Peter 5:8 says, "Be sober, be vigilant; because your adversary the devil walks about like a roaring lion, seeking whom he may devour. We can see that Scripture teaches us that Satan walks about as a roaring lion seeking whom he may devour and at times does so appearing as an angel of light. The devil craves worship after being cast out of heaven and actually before, thus his rebellion. Isaiah14:12-15 "How you are fallen from heaven, O Lucifer, son of the morning! How you are cut down to the ground, you who weakened the nations! For you have said in your heart: 'I will ascend into heaven, I will exalt my throne above the stars of God; I will also sit on the mount of the congregation on the farthest sides of the north; I will ascend above the heights of the clouds, I will be like the Most High.' Yet you shall be brought down to Sheol, to the lowest depths of the pit."

Do not be deceived into worshipping angels and thereby lose the prize you hope for like they did in Colossians 2:18 "Let no one cheat you of your reward, taking delight in false humility and worship of angels, intruding into those things which he has not seen."

As the rulers of this world proclaim there is no God or that God is dead and the people agree, the demonic spirit of Jezebel rules. The spirit of Jezebel desires to shut the mouths of the prophets who proclaim the word of God in order to further perpetuate the lie, among her other ungodly traits. (First and Second Kings) Declaring there is no God and agreeing with that declaration leaves the craving for the supernatural things of God that He created in man from the beginning, to become an open vacuum for the ploys of the enemy. As these deceived people seek to fill that longing, they begin to suck in and believe any appearance of the supernatural as truth. Satan is all too happy to fill it with "angels of light" among other cunning strategies to deceive and hold captive as many people on the earth that he is able.

Satan knows his time on earth is short before God hands down his final judgment and punishment, and being evil, he wants to take down as many as he can before that time. Even as he went around to God's angels and deceived one-third of them to be on his side for the rebellion that got them all cast out of heaven, he does so with mankind. This is a counterfeit of the Son who wishes to bring salvation to mankind through His love. Satan's goal is to counterfeit everything of God, to deceive the people. This is why it is vital to understand what God's angels do and what they do not do. Because of Satan's plan of deception, his fallen angels are all too happy to lead mankind astray by tricking whomever they can into believing they are "God's angels" thereby leading them into captivity.

Thank you, Father God, for giving us Jesus, the Truth, who came to set the captives free!

CHAPTER EIGHT
UNDERSTANDING SPIRITUAL WARFARE

In this chapter, I'll share with you the most awesome angelic encounter I have ever been blessed with and how it led me to understand spiritual warfare in a way I never did before. But in reading the scripture God sent the angel to deliver to me, revelation came through His Holy Spirit, and understanding was granted to me to share for such a time as this.

As was routine for me, I was sitting on the floor of my bedroom with my Bible and note pad as I prayed and studied the Word. I had been praying in the Spirit for a while and began seeking God as to which scripture he wanted me to study. Suddenly the area around me appeared white as if I were in wispy clouds. I saw the bottom of a radiantly white robe with a bright gold design embroidered along the bottom of the hem.

Thinking Jesus appeared, I instantly fell lower on the floor and began to worship him when an authoritative voice spoke saying, "Do not worship me as I am a messenger of the Lord!" He then told me the Lord wanted me to read in Ephesians 6 about the armor of God. Then, just as quickly as he had appeared, he disappeared.

Although I had read those scriptures many times, I turned over to them in my Bible to be obedient to my Lord's wishes and began to read Ephesians 6, starting at verse 10 and received revelation concerning those scriptures I hadn't realized before.

"Finally, my brethren, be strong in the Lord and in the power of His might. Put on the whole armor of God that you may be able to stand against the wiles of the devil. For we do not wrestle against flesh and blood, but against principalities, against powers, against rulers of the darkness of this age, against spiritual hosts of wickedness in the heavenly places. Therefore, take up the whole armor of God that you may be able to withstand in the evil day, and having done all, to stand. Stand therefore, having girded your waist with truth."

At this point, I prayed, "Lord, I am girded with the truth. Jesus said He is the way, the truth and the life. I have accepted him as my savior and invited him to be Lord of my life. I believe your truth over the lies of the enemy. Satan tries to make me believe that I am a hopeless sinner, lost and defeated, unloved and without hope. But I know he is the father of all lies and the truth is not in him. I know Jesus said I would know the truth and the truth would set me free. I have girded my waist with the truth, I am girded with Jesus."

I continued on, "having put on the breastplate of righteousness,"

I prayed, "Lord, I know the breastplate in a suit of armor covers the heart and I have given my heart to you. I know that I am righteous because of Jesus' righteousness and not of my own self. The way into your kingdom is not by any works of man, but by your Spirit, lest any man should boast. It is the righteousness of Jesus that covers me and protects my heart from all of Satan's false accusations. I know that when you said in Ezekiel 36:26-27 'I will give you a new heart and put a new spirit within you; I will take the heart of stone out of your flesh and give you a heart of flesh. I will put My Spirit within you and cause you to walk in My statutes, and you will keep My judgments and do them.', that you gave me a heart transplant and it now flows with the blood of the lamb. Thank you for the heart of Jesus."

I read on "and having shod your feet with the preparation of the gospel of peace;"

"Lord", I prayed, "I have your peace, the peace you gave me that passes all understanding. I trust you in every situation. I am following you wherever you lead me to go and sharing of your goodness and love. You have placed me on a path I walk with you with sure footedness because as in Isaiah 9:6 'For unto us a Child is born, unto us a son is given; and the government will be upon his shoulder. And His name will be called Wonderful, Counselor, Mighty God, Everlasting Father, Prince of Peace.' Or in other words, His name will be called Jesus."

Next, I read, "Above all, taking the shield of faith with which, you will be able to quench all the fiery darts of the wicked one."

I prayed, "Lord, you know of my faith, of how I have believed You and Your Word and in Jesus, Your Son who sacrificed his life, so that I could have eternal life since I was just a little girl. I know that You have given me the gift of faith and brought me through many a storm, trial, and numerous tribulations causing that faith to grow up into a shield, protecting me from the attacks of the enemy. It is you Lord, who are my shield as Psalm 33:20 says, 'Our soul waits for the LORD; He is our help and our shield.'"

I returned to the scriptures reading, "And take the helmet of salvation."

"Lord, I know our salvation comes through Jesus and the helmet protects our head that harbors our brain, our mind, like in Second Corinthians 10:3-5 'For though we walk in the flesh, we do not war according to the flesh. For the weapons of our warfare are not carnal but mighty in God for pulling down strongholds, casting down arguments and every high thing that exalts itself against the knowledge of God, bringing every thought into captivity to the obedience of Christ', of Jesus. Our mind is where we are tempted by the enemy and resist him with scripture, the Word of God, just as Jesus did in the wilderness. The Word of God in the flesh is Jesus."

I continued reading, "and the sword of the Spirit, which is the Word of God…" Suddenly, I couldn't see my Bible anymore because a bright white mist began to swirl over it and around me. I blinked my eyes and when I opened them, I was surrounded by it. Somehow, I just knew I was in the midst of clouds. I was suspended, sort of like just hanging there with no solid ground I could stand on. I couldn't see the Lord, but sensed His presence behind me.

Before I even had time to contemplate that, a black being appeared before me and a fear like I have never experienced before came over me, paralyzing me. This being was the blackest black I had ever seen. I couldn't make out the features of its face as they were set back beneath what appeared to me as some sort of black helmet. The being had bright red glowing eyes though and that is all I could make out except the evil and hatred radiating from it. I couldn't see the form of its body because both of us were in the midst of whirling clouds. My heart was pounding so hard, it was shaking my whole body with every beat.

All of a sudden, this creature held up a black sword and swung it forward and back, slicing the air as if in a taunt. I could not believe this whole situation and was so frightened. I don't know how I knew, but I just knew that this evil being desired to kill me, truly meant to kill me! I was so scared and felt so all alone, like I had been deserted and left to die. The black being raised up its sword again and then I heard a voice instruct me to not be afraid and to wield my sword of the Spirit. It was in that moment I noticed a bright and shiny silver double-edged sword in my hand. As I looked at it, I saw it flash from a sword to my Bible, and back to a sword again.

The creature which I had determined at this point was demonic, swung his sword and as it did, a stream I can best describe as a lime green glowing laser light with fire and electrical currents snapping and crackling within it shot out from the tip toward me. It was like the color green that represents toxic waste. I instinctively lifted up my sword, saw it turn into my Bible again, and as the laser beam hit my Bible, it was shattered into a ton of tiny sparks that fell away and disappeared. This gave me some courage.

I raised my sword up and as I swung it at the creature, a stream of red, yellow and orange fire came forth from my tip and shot forth toward the demon. This infuriated it and I tangibly felt its anger rage toward me even more. It swung its sword and again and the toxic green laser came toward me and again my sword turned into my Bible in my hand and blocked the attack of the enemy. Each time this happened, its swings came closer and closer together as its anger and hatred intensified further still. It moved closer toward me and I stepped back wielding my interchanging Bible sword. We went around and around faster and faster lunging toward each other with our swords in battle and me blocking its intended death blows with my only weapon, my Bible sword.

I don't know how long this battle took place with me suspended in the heavenlies, but thank you Jesus, the demon was defeated and disappeared. Upon its disappearance, I felt myself falling for a split second and then landing on my bed as if I had been dropped. I could barely catch my breath. My lungs were burning with every inhalation of breath. It felt just like the time in seventh grade gym class after we had to run around the whole football field five times.

I was exhausted and my muscles felt like jelly. My clothes were soaking wet from sweat and clinging to my body. My hair was plastered to my head, also saturated in sweat. My heart was pounding within my chest walls and I could do nothing but replay in my mind what had happened and wonder how my body was physically fatigued and how I started out praying and studying my Bible on the floor but was now lying on my bed.

The only thing I knew with certainty was that I had just experienced something spiritual, something supernatural and yet physical at the same time. However, I had no idea how that could be. I also knew that the Bible truly is living and powerful and sharper than any two-edged sword, that God's Word is truth and therefore consequently powerful. I understood that the sword of God's Word both protects us and destroys the enemy, defeating Satan and his temptation attempts toward us. I knew it made sense because after all, the Word of God is exactly how Jesus defeated Satan's temptation in the wilderness. Jesus defeated Satan by quoting the Word of God with each of the temptations Satan presented Him with in Matthew 4:1-11. But as for the physical part, I didn't understand and was perplexed.

As I later contemplated upon this supernatural experience, I realized all I had prayed as I read the scriptures as instructed by the angel, I had likened each piece of the armor of God to Jesus. I got my Bible out and began to search the scriptures and sure enough, it's in there! Roman's 13:11-14 "And do this, knowing the time, that now it is high time to awake out of sleep; for now, our salvation is nearer than when we first believed. The night is far spent, the day is at hand. Therefore, let us cast off the works of darkness, and let us put on the armor of light. Let us walk properly, as in the day, not in revelry and drunkenness, not in lewdness and lust, not in strife and envy. But put on the Lord Jesus Christ, and make no provision for the flesh, to fulfill its lust."

As I read that last line, "But put on the Lord Jesus Christ, and make no provision for the flesh, to fulfill its lust", I suddenly understood the meaning of the natural part of my body being involved in this otherwise spiritual warfare experience that had so befuddled me. Although we do not wrestle against flesh and blood, but against principalities, against powers, against rulers of the darkness of this age, against spiritual hosts of wickedness in the heavenly places, we do wrestle with our own flesh.

Galatians chapter 5 explains this perfectly in verses 16 and 17. "I say then: Walk in the Spirit, and you shall not fulfill the lust of the flesh. For the flesh lusts against the Spirit, and the Spirit against the flesh; and these two are contrary to one another, so that you do not do the things that you wish." Apostle Paul also shared, explaining this battle in Romans, chapter 7, "For what I will to do, I do not practice; but what I hate, that I do." This again reiterates the battle we have between our spirit and our flesh, our carnal selves or our sin nature.

I understood my body was drenched in sweat and fatigued representing that we live on this earth in the flesh, that our spirit is housed in flesh while we physically serve and toil for the Lord. We must battle our flesh just as Jesus did before sacrificing Himself on the cross. In Luke chapter 22, we find Jesus in agony, so He prayed more earnestly. Then His sweat became like blood, falling to the ground. Jesus had to battle His flesh man so His spirit man would win. He could have called upon God the father to send Him twelve legions of angels as He says in Matthew 26:52, but He didn't. Rather, Jesus continued praying, asking His Father to let the cup pass from Him if it were possible, but in the end said, "Yet not as I will, but as you will." During this intense battle, Jesus taught the disciples to pray lest they fall into temptation saying for the spirit is willing, but the flesh is weak.

Jesus himself had to battle his flesh and carnal mind before going to the cross. He knew it would be painful. He knew He would be beaten until He was barely recognizable. He knew that He then, in that near death weakened condition, would have to drag His cross to the place of crucifixion. He knew how painful the Roman crucifixion was and exactly what it entailed. Of course, His flesh, the part of Him that was fully human, didn't want to do that. His spirit wanted to though because He knew that by giving His life on the cross and shedding His blood, He was giving to everyone the ability to be forgiven and receive eternal life. He knew it was the will of Father God. Only through prayer could He get His spirit stronger than His flesh. The same is true of us.

The devil is not out to get us per se', but rather out to get us to get our own selves by giving into our sin nature through the temptations he brings, leading us into sin, the very thing that separates us from God. Just like the serpent tempted Adam and Eve in the Garden of Eden leading to the very first sin. Satan started tempting way back then and has not stopped. The struggle is real. We war against our flesh wanting to be selfish and do what brings it pleasure leading to spiritual death, and our spirit man doing what God asks of us to do. We don't war on our own, but by prayer that builds up our faith, and by Jesus who gives us the strength to do all things in Him. He overcame all and as we conquer our carnal mind, will, and emotions, truly becoming Christ like, we will too. Not by ourselves, but by Jesus who is in us and by putting on Christ Jesus. It's that simple but it is in no way, shape, or form, easy.

Allow me a pause, to further explain what God revealed. In following the moves of God in the church, the restorations and revelations He brings, we can always see a pendulum swing. It is first too far to the left, then swings too far to the right, but with time, becomes centered.

The same is true with spiritual warfare. When revelation was brought forth that we have power over the enemy, power over Satan and his fallen hordes, we began to swing too far to the right with our focus being on demons as opposed to prior to, not or barely recognizing the power we have over them, which was the swing of the far left. The church was excited about this knowledge and began to teach about it causing her to focus on the demonic.

I know from experience, whatever you focus on, you see. Whenever we got a new car, all of a sudden, I was seeing that same make and model of car everywhere. They didn't just suddenly appear, however. They were always there, but because my mind was now more focused on that particular make and model, I saw them. The same thing happened in the body of Christ when that revelation of power over the enemy was brought forth. Demons were being found in abundance and the church was engaging in spiritual warfare, exercising their newfound power over them. Satan was all too happy to comply in sending demons, thereby keeping the church's focus on demons more so than on God.

Philippians 4:8 tells us where our focus should be. "Finally, brethren, whatever things are true, whatever things are noble, whatever things are just, whatever things are pure, whatever things are lovely, whatever things are of good report, if there is any virtue and if there is anything praiseworthy – meditate on these things". Those things Paul described to the Philippians most certainly do not describe Satan and his demons, therefore our focus should not be on them, but be on the things of God. Luke 10:17-20 says, "Then the seventy returned with joy, saying, 'Lord, even the demons are subject to us in Your name.' And He said to them, 'I saw Satan fall like lightening from heaven. Behold, I give you the authority to trample on serpents and scorpions, and over all the power of the enemy, and nothing shall by any means hurt you. Nevertheless, do not rejoice in this, that the spirits are subject to you, but rather rejoice because your names are written in heaven.'" Here Jesus is teaching us that our focus should be on the things of God, rather than on the demons.

Being sons of God, joint heirs with Christ and brothers of Jesus, we need to follow His example in Luke chapter 2. After the Feast of Passover in Jerusalem, Mary and Joseph along with their company, headed home and thought Jesus who was 12 years of age, was among them. But after traveling a whole day, they realized He wasn't and then backtracked to find Him. After searching for three more days, they found Him in the Temple speaking with teachers. When they inquired why He stayed behind and worried them, He responded with a question and asked, "Did you not know that I must be about my Father's business?" Just as Jesus was about the Kingdom of God while he walked the earth, we are to do also.

We should give praise to God because now the pendulum swing is being centered in the understanding that the battle is God's, not ours. We only need to resist the devil and he will flee. When we are focused on God the Father, God the Son, and God the Holy Spirit, putting on Jesus, being the light bearers in the midst of a crooked and perverse generation, resisting the devil's temptations by the Word of God, we've got the devil fleeing from us. He wants to avoid us at all costs as he recognizes our authority over him by recognizing Jesus in and on us. In other words, he identifies Jesus, who already defeated him, and beats it out of there.

Second Chronicles 20:15 says "…for the battle is not yours, but God's." Also, when we are light bearers, heaven and earth converge. The light of Jesus we carry on earth converges with heaven, from whence our light comes, thereby piercing the darkness between the two. Therefore, there are no principalities, powers, rulers of darkness, or hosts of wickedness in the heavenlies as they had to flee from us and the light we carry.

It is very much like what is referred to as Jacob's ladder in Genesis 28:10-13. Jacob takes a stone for a pillow and falls asleep. He then has a dream where there is a ladder set up on the earth and its top reached to heaven and angels of God were going up and down it. Then in verses 16 and 17, Jacob wakes up and says, "Surely the LORD is in this place and I did not know it. How awesome is this place! This is none other than the house of God, and this place is the gate of heaven." This is very similar to what happens as each and every child of God, the sons of God, put on Christ Jesus, the armor of light. Heaven and earth converge and nothing of darkness can stand in the light. Hallelujah! Thank you, Lord!

Furthermore, once we conquer the flesh through Jesus, we will then have the love that produced the compassion Father God had for us when he gave us Jesus, and the love that fashioned the compassion Jesus had for us that caused the battle between His flesh and spirit, that motivated Him to do God's will and give His life for us on the cross. The Father's love and compassion that led Jesus to pray to the Father, "Father, forgive them, for they know not what they do." We will examine God's perfect love in more depth in an upcoming chapter, as it is a multi-faceted love, requiring in depth study.

CHAPTER NINE
SUPERNATURAL MANIFESTATIONS

As I hear the Spirit say the time of increased supernatural manifestations is at hand, I first want to share with you the times God intervened supernaturally in my life as He has asked of me, thereby showing you a few of the different ways God moves in them.

The very first supernatural manifestation I recall was after I had moved back in with my mom. I was eighteen years old and enjoying the freedom that comes with owning one's first car. My mom had given it to me as a graduation gift. When I tell you it was silver and rust, know that silver was the color of the paint and rust was not, but rather the condition. That didn't matter to me, I had a car that ran and could get me places I wanted to go without relying on anybody else. I was genuinely thankful.

Being a typical teenage girl, one of my passions was shopping. After payday each week, I would go to the shopping mall a few towns over and buy myself something new, mostly clothing of some sort or another. This particular day, I had bought myself a new pair of jeans and a new colorful long-sleeved top. I was eager to wear my new outfit this coming weekend as I hung out with the girls uptown. I was on my way home, window down, wind blowing through my hair and music playing, well, blasting actually, on the radio as I approached the flashing light at the intersection.

The light in my direction flashed yellow, while the other direction flashed red. It was early afternoon on a weekday and so traffic was very light. As I was drawing near the light, I spotted an eighteen-wheeler semi-truck speeding up to the intersection. I knew he had no intentions of stopping at his red flashing light. I also realized, as I saw the shock and fear in the driver's eyes as he spotted me, that neither he nor I would be able to stop in time.

Natural instinct took over and I immediately slammed on the brakes as hard as I could. I closed my eyes because I didn't want to see the crash that would cause my death. I felt my car begin to fishtail and then straighten out. I heard the squealing of my tires. I kept my eyes closed and body tense awaiting the inevitable. But there was no impact, no crash. I couldn't believe it, so I opened my eyes only to find myself in the middle of the intersection and that semi-truck already through it. "No way!" my brain screamed in my head as it registered there was no way that could have happened without divine intervention.

I honestly don't remember the rest of the way home. I think I was in mild shock. What I do remember is pulling up in the driveway, falling out of the car prostrate onto the gravel and thanking God for saving my life while tears of gratitude and thanksgiving streamed down my face. I stayed there lying in the driveway for what seemed like hours until my heart slowed and my body quit uncontrollably shaking.

In retrospect, I do wish I would have kept my eyes open so I could have seen what actually happened. Was there an angel who stood in front of my car to keep me from proceeding through the intersection? Did God's hand or blast of His nostril cause that tractor trailer to supernaturally, in lightning speed, race through? Did God pick up the semi and put it down on the other side of the flashing light? I honestly don't know, but what I do know is a supernatural manifestation undeniably occurred and if it hadn't, I would not be alive today. Of that, I have no doubt and am more thankful than my words can express.

Another supernatural manifestation occurred in my life with the birth of my son. Shortly after returning home with my second daughter, I was overcome with a high fever that weakened me so much I could barely get out of bed to take care of my new baby and firstborn daughter. After taking my temperature and seeing the reading of 104.3, I called my doctor and he told me to get to the hospital immediately. I called Bill and after dropping off our oldest at my grandmother's house, we went to emergency. It turns out, after giving birth to our second child, part of the placenta had not been removed and it caused an infection in my whole pelvic area. I was hospitalized for ten days with an I.V. drip of a broad-spectrum antibiotic after the removal of the rest of the placenta. Bill was such a sweetheart as he brought up both our daughters to visit me during that time. Finally, I was released to go home.

But shortly thereafter, I began getting sharp stabbing pains in the pelvic area that dropped me to my knees. My doctor ordered a laparoscopy where he would go in with a micro camera through a small incision below my belly button. He explained he would be able to see what was going on and be able to fix whatever he found while he was in. Upon waking from the anesthesia, he told me he had some good news and some bad news for me. He started with the good news and told me the infection I had after birth had caused a lot of scar tissue and that scar tissue had grown and attached my fallopian tubes to my abdominal wall. The good news was that he was able to detach them so I shouldn't have those sharp stabbing pains anymore.

The bad news came next. My doctor explained that the infection I had incurred was very much like Pelvic Inflammatory Disease with the difference being it didn't result from a sexually transmitted disease. However, the results were the same. The infection was so bad and everywhere in my pelvic region that everything was now affected with scar tissue. He further explained that my fimbriae at the end of my fallopian tubes, the small, fingerlike projections through which eggs move from the ovaries to the uterus were no longer functional. They were now the equivalent of duck feet and couldn't do their intended job. But there's more. Both of my fallopian tubes were over ninety percent blocked with scar tissue meaning I couldn't become pregnant again and if by chance I did, I would have an ectopic pregnancy that could kill me if not discovered in time.

Needless to say, I was devastated. Although I loved my daughters dearly, I did want to have a son. Without one, the Kern name would end with Bill. I also knew that Bill wanted a son as well. Our second daughter was born close to his birthday and he had confided in me that not only would he like for the baby to be born on his birthday, but he wanted it to be a boy and named after him. I laughed and exclaimed I thought he asked too much. Anyway, none of those wishes came to fruition. Neither Bill nor I spoke of our desire to have a son after that as it was just too painful. However, my silent prayers persisted.

And then God! About two years later, I had just woken up and was making my way to the living room when I heard a voice in my right ear say, "You are going to bear a son." I instantly looked all around me to see if someone was in the house in an attempt to identify where that voice came from, still being very groggy from sleep. Of course, there was no one there. I knew right then and there I had heard from God. I was so excited. I couldn't wait for Bill to come home from work and share this awesome news with him.

For the next six months, Bill and I tried to conceive, but month after month, there was no pregnancy. I was so distraught with failure after failure. I felt I just couldn't take it anymore. I then told Bill I was putting the kibosh on trying to get pregnant, that I just couldn't go through the disappointment any longer. Then, wouldn't you just know it. Three weeks later, I missed my monthly cycle. I went out and bought a home pregnancy test and tested positive. I was so elated! The next step was making an appointment with my doctor.

After several different tests, my doctor declared to me that I was indeed pregnant, and it was a normal pregnancy. Everything was as it should be. I then said, "But I thought you said I was infertile and couldn't have any more children." He responded by telling me that he was only human and not God. He asked me to trust him and finished with the declaration that for me to have a normal pregnancy was indeed an act of God, for it was a medical impossibility. Praise God and thank you Jesus for giving Bill and I the desire of our hearts, because in June the following year, I gave birth to a healthy baby boy! God intervened supernaturally and overturned a barren womb into one that brought forth a son, causing even a physician to declare the handiwork of God Almighty!

God is a God of miracles. He always has been and always will be. God's people have been experiencing miracles in their lives since God created man back in the beginning. We learn of these all throughout the Old and New Testaments and therefore, it's no wonder that His people still experience them today.

When we look back through the Scriptures, we see miracles in people's bodies as they are raised from the dead, total body healings, and miracles dealing with nature. Some examples are the star over Bethlehem, the Red Sea parting, a donkey talking to a prophet, a bird coming and feeding a prophet, earthquakes and droughts, darkness as the sun doesn't shine when it should and see the sun shining when it shouldn't, as a few examples. We see a man being delivered where God wants Him via a large fish. We see a man being transported where God wants him to be, instantaneously. We see infestations of animals and crops and things that go against nature. These all are supernatural manifestations God brought about. Some were on a personal basis, some on a local basis, and some on a regional basis. But there was only one on a global basis and that is when God caused it to rain for forty days and forty nights, flooding the entire globe. It is the story of Noah's ark.

Genesis 6: 9 says, "Noah was a just man, perfect in his generations. Noah walked with God." Verses 11-14 reads, "The earth was also corrupt before God and the earth was filled with violence. So, God looked upon the earth and indeed it was corrupt; for all flesh had corrupted the way on earth. And God said to Noah, 'The end of all flesh has come before Me, for the earth is filled with violence through them; and behold, I will destroy them with the earth. Make yourself an ark…'"

In Genesis 7:1 we find, "Then the Lord said to Noah, 'Come into the ark, you and all your household, because I have seen that you are righteous before Me in this generation.'" We see in verse 4 God continuing, "For after seven more days I will cause it to rain on the earth forty days and forty nights." We know Noah obeyed God and collected two of every creature and put them on the ark in obedience to God's word. Verse 16 tells us once they were all in, "The Lord shut him in."

When The Lord had finished all He said He would accomplish, Noah and his family were able to disembark and start over with a covenant from God and a promise not to curse the ground for man's sake, although the imagination of man's heart is evil from his youth: nor again destroy every living thing as He had done.

This was a global supernatural manifestation. The next global supernatural manifestation we find, is the life, death and resurrection of Jesus. This is God's supernatural manifestation working to be global, as to the ends of the earth. Or in other words, it's a supernatural WIP, (work in progress). And when the work is complete, then the end will come. In Acts 1:8 Jesus says, "But you shall receive power when the Holy Spirit has come upon you; and you shall be witnesses to Me in Jerusalem, and in all Judea and Samaria, and to the end of the earth. Jesus also says to His disciples in Matthew 24:14 "And this gospel of the kingdom will be preached in all the world as a witness to all the nations, and then the end will come."

I hear the Spirit saying that this is a new time, a time for new anointing, a time for increase, a time where He will do new things, and we cannot even imagine the things He has planned for the earth and its inhabitants as His ways are higher than ours and His thoughts higher than ours. But know this; they will be blessings mighty and awesome to His people. And to remember that blessings don't always come wrapped in beautiful gift wrap that makes us "ooh and ahh" as we would want or prefer, however, the gift inside is priceless. Know that He will do many mighty things by His hand, with the blast of His nostrils, and through the hands of his anointed vessels who heed His call and answer, Yes Lord! I do hear the Spirit say this is a phase where we will see an increase in supernatural manifestations and some will be on an individual level, some will be local, some will be regional, and some will be global. We are a global world now and it need be for God to accomplish His Works not only in the earth, but in us, His willing vessels.

May we be encouraged by Second Peter 3:8-9, "But beloved, do not forget this one thing, that with the Lord one day is as a thousand years, and a thousand years as one day. The Lord is not slack concerning His promise, as some count slackness, but is longsuffering toward us, not willing that any should perish but that all should come to repentance."

Yes Lord! Amen and amen!

CHAPTER TEN
THE COURSE OF THIS WORLD

Scripture tells us that we are to be aware of and be separate from the course of this world, the spirit of the age, and the ways of the world, for they are the enemy of God and His children. We find examples of this in the following scriptures.

Ephesians 2:1-2 "And you He made alive, who were dead in trespasses and sin, in which you once walked according to the course of this world, according to the prince of the power of the air, the spirit who now works in the sons of disobedience…"

First Corinthians 2 verses 6 and 12 - Verse 6 says, "However, we speak wisdom among those who are mature, yet not the wisdom of this age, who are coming to nothing." And verse 12 says, "Now we have received, not the spirit of the world, but the Spirit who is from God…"

James 4:4 "…Do you not know that friendship with the world is enmity with God?"

The course of the world, also known as the spirit of the age, has changed throughout history in different and sundry times. We do need to understand what the course of our age is in order to comprehend where we are today. We can simply look out into society while using scripture as our measuring device to discover it. In the books of Timothy, we find the pulse of our present societal world.

First Timothy 4:1-5 KJV "Now the Spirit speaketh expressly, that in the latter times some shall depart from the faith, giving heed to seducing spirits, and doctrines of devils; speaking lies in hypocrisy; having their conscience seared with a hot iron; forbidding to marry, and commanding to abstain from meats, which God hath created to be received with thanksgiving of them which believe and know the truth. For every creature of God is good, and nothing to be refused, if it be received with thanksgiving: For it is sanctified by the word of God and prayer.

Here we find some clues. "Departing from the faith" …Unfortunately, today many refer to the precious good news of Jesus' life, death and resurrection as a 2000-year-old fairy tale. "giving heed to seducing spirits, and doctrines of devils; speaking lies in hypocrisy;" What is being spread all over is that all paths lead to God and heaven, that everyone goes to heaven when they die, so it doesn't matter which "religion" they choose to follow in life. We have some religions teaching things contrary to the word of God, but we know that there is only one way to the Father and that is through Jesus. We know our sins are forgiven by confessing them and then we are cleansed through the blood of the lamb. First John 1:9 says, "If we confess our sins, He is faithful and just to forgive us our sins and to cleanse us from all unrighteousness." We know that confession and repentance takes seeing our sin the same way God does. It's not just a little mantra to repeat. It's a matter of the heart. True repentance brings about a change of heart as the heart of stone is made flesh by His Spirit.

Continuing on we see, "having their conscience seared with a hot iron; forbidding to marry," When the world says those things God has deemed as sin is okay and even made into law sometimes, we know consciences have been seared. We also see marriage deteriorating and couples living together and referring to each other as significant others, life partners, and the like, even between couples of the same sex, with society seeing this as perfectly acceptable. Killing babies while they are still in the womb and throwing them out as trash, the very lives God has breathed His Spirit into, is seen as progress. Lastly, from this scripture, we find, "and commanding to abstain from meats, which God hath created to be received with thanksgiving of them which believe and know the truth. For every creature of God is good, and nothing to be refused, if it be received with thanksgiving: For it is sanctified by the word of God and prayer."

Right now, vegetarianism and veganism are popular. We see a new wave of "meatless" menus in restaurants and fast food joints. People are refusing to eat meat because they believe the animals from which we get our meat that Father God gave us to feed, nourish and strengthen our bodies, are equals to humans who God created in His own image and breathed His Spirit into. They have delegated the sanctity of our lives to the creatures of the earth and lifted the creatures of the earth to the same level as us, God's children. And all He asks is that we will say blessing over our food, including meat, in thanksgiving, for it to be healthy for our bodies. A certain sign of the times!

Now let's take a look at Second Timothy 3:1-4 "But know this, that in the last days perilous times will come: For men will be lovers of themselves, lovers of money, boasters, proud, blasphemers, disobedient to parents, unthankful, unholy, unloving, unforgiving, slanderers, without self-control, brutal, despisers of good, having a form of godliness but denying its power…"

Let's discuss two of the themes running through this scripture. The first being selfishness. We'll discuss just a few examples of this just so you can begin to see the pulse. When we look out into the world, we can definitely see the world pulse as having passion for pleasure, power, privilege, and proceeds, all of which tie into selfishness. People are thinking of themselves before others, or put in other words, "it's all about me". This isn't surprising to see as it has been building up for quite a few decades. Recently, there was the cute little bunny with the saying "It's all about me" all over on social media, notebooks, t-shirts, coffee mugs, etc. This was conditioning minds to think that way. The program in the schools of no child left behind, rewarding everyone with trophies, ribbons and even grades without the children having to put in any work. This in turn gave them a sense of entitlement leading to selfishness. In making life all about themselves and what they want and feel, has produced a slew of mental disorders. We see hoarding, depression, deep anger, and narcissism as a few examples.

Alcoholism, suicide, drug addiction and overdose, are at all-time highs as some begin to realize that the rest of the world isn't making it all about them, and then try to soothe their feelings of inadequacy from it. Obviously, if you're only thinking of yourself, you don't love your neighbor as yourself as the Scriptures tell us we are to do. They'll then argue, fight, harden their heart, create dissention, gossip, rail against others, lose control of themselves, and the list goes on and on. All of this is unmistakably the opposite of walking in God's love.

In addition, because of all of the above problems, secular humanistic counseling has become a billion-dollar industry. To me, as we see in Isaiah 9:6 "For unto us a Child is born, unto us a son is given; and the government will be upon his shoulder. And His name will be called Wonderful, Counselor, Mighty God, Everlasting Father, Prince of Peace.", the saddest thing about people paying for secular counseling is that Jesus is the wonderful Counselor and His counseling is free. Scripture tells us it is God who gives us a sound mind. Christian counselors are acceptable as long as they don't deny God's power to heal and make whole. If they rely solely on secular counseling without the power of Jesus' healing blood and name, it is an example of having a form of godliness, but denying its power, which brings us to the next theme.

"...having a form of godliness but denying its power." We must understand that any religion and I use this term loosely, that does not teach the truth, the whole truth, and nothing but the truth of the Word, is denying the power of God. In First John we learn that the Word is God and was with God and the Word became flesh and dwelt among us. Clearly, the Word is Jesus. Yes, the whole Bible is Jesus and so if you leave parts out or permit things that are not permissible in the Holy Scriptures, then that is not fully Jesus and therefore, has a form of godliness, but denies the power of God.

Unfortunately, many religions, in the name of tolerance, are becoming very popular. They call themselves godly but aren't in the sense we just explained. One such example is a gathering that describes itself as being for people who might call themselves spiritual but not religious. It is for those who sense the depths of their own being and celebrate the awareness of a power greater than themselves. These teachings bring together ancient wisdom with new interpretations of what it means to be alive and human and inspire different ways to think about the force of love and intelligence that many people call God. It encourages you to live the truth you know and not the truth, the way and the life. This is completely contrary to the Word and seems to mirror some of the false religions spoken about all throughout the Scriptures, and perhaps, even all of them. What is very concerning is that if everything is permissible, then no one has to be accountable for anything, and the holiness we are called to walk in is obsolete, not to mention never being able to come to maturity.

Don't be deceived! Paul warns us in First Corinthians 6:9-10 not to walk after the ways of the world and its courts and laws to weigh what is righteous. "Do you not know that the unrighteous will not inherit the kingdom of God? Do not be deceived. Neither fornicators, nor idolaters, nor adulterers, nor homosexuals, nor sodomites, nor thieves, nor covetous, nor drunkards, nor revilers, nor extortioners will inherit the kingdom of God." Period!

Now let's take a look at Second Timothy 4:3-4 "For the time will come when they will not endure sound doctrine, but according to their own desires, because they have itching ears, they will heap up for themselves teachers; and they will turn their ears away from the truth, and be turned aside to fables."

We are seeing this take off like wildfire in our society today. Some are looking to science to be their god. I'm sure we've all heard of the religion that proclaims we come from aliens and they are going to come back and reclaim us some day, brought about by archeological digs and so-called discoveries. Itch in the ear scratched.

One of the more recent "heaped up" teachers embraced, to soothe the itch, was a scientist revered as the most intelligent scientific mind of all times, even having held a seat once occupied by Sir Isaac Newton. He was even venerated for speaking nonsensical proclamations and so many ate it up and ran with it. He proclaimed, "I regard the brain as a computer which will stop working when its components fail. There is no heaven or afterlife for broken down computers; that is a fairy story for people afraid of the dark."

And as if that wasn't bad enough, this scientist later proclaimed, "Because there is a law such as gravity, the universe can and will create itself from nothing. Spontaneous creation is the reason there is something rather than nothing, why the universe exists, why we exist." These proclamations are wrong on so many levels when measured with the Word of God. Anyone with a sound mind knows that if one would take this as fact and step off the top of a two story barn, because of the law of gravity, the spectacular thing that would be spontaneously created would be a fall resulting in broken bones and internal injuries, if not death. Yet, so many have now embraced the universe as their god. Apparently, worshipping the stars got too small as scientific knowledge increased and allowed men to see farther into space, so that now, worship has been expanded to the universe.

In many varied types of media, we are hearing references to the universe "giving signs" to people. An online friend of mine after seeing my life full of blessings and answered prayer, from that false religion angle, proclaimed that the universe liked me. No, no, no! The Creator of the universe loves me! I also recently had an old schoolmate relate to me after I shared my faith with him that he believes the universe created us, put us on this planet, and left us on our own, not caring one iota about us. It breaks my heart to see people believe and proclaim this. Why worship the created universe when you can praise and worship and have a personal relationship, walking and talking with the very One who created and rules the universe? I continue to pray for him and can't even imagine what kind of hurt he experienced in his life to bring him to that conclusion.

In continuing on in Second Timothy 3, verse 4 "...And from such people, turn away." Then Timothy hits on what we just discussed regarding science. In verse 7 he says, "...always learning and never able to come to the knowledge of the truth." I think this perfectly covers the increasing study and intelligence regarding the sciences and resulting technology and fits it to a "T".

When I was looking out at society to gain the perspective of the pulse, the thing that really struck me was all of the arguing and disrespect there is over politics and elected officials, the worst of all being "not my President". This mockery is not only found in social media, but on most news broadcasts and other media outlets too. So, I began to search the scriptures regarding this and what I discovered really made my jaw drop to my chin as the revelation became clear. Back in Isaiah 9:6, this phrase jumped out at me. "...and the government will be upon his shoulder..." When Jesus was given to us by the Father as prophesied about in Isaiah, He was referred to as King. We know this from Matthew 2:2. Here, we find the wise men inquiring "Where is He who has been born King of the Jews?" Jesus was referred to as King of kings and Lord of lords because of what was written over His head upon the cross of crucifixion. Also, Timothy in First Timothy 6:15 says, "which He will manifest in His own time, He who is blessed and only Potentate, the King of kings and Lord of lords...". We also know that kings rule and therefore are government.

I couldn't find in the New Testament any place where Jesus or his disciples spoke ill of or criticized the cruel, oppressive Roman government. What I did find, was where the Pharisees were trying to trip Jesus up and asked Jesus if they should pay taxes to Caesar. See, they were aware that all things belong to God for in Job 41:11, God asked Job, "But who has preceded Me that I should pay him? Everything under heaven is Mine." So, Jesus asked for a coin and asked them whose image was on the coin. When they answered it was Caesar's, Jesus answered them back and told them to render onto Caesar what is Caesar's and unto God what is God's, in Luke chapter 20:20-25. Jesus showed they should be obedient to the government leader. Roman's 13: 1-2 teaches us to," Let every soul be subject to the governing authorities. For there is no authority except from God, therefore whoever resists the authority resists the ordinance of God, and those who resist will bring judgment upon themselves." Wow!

All governmental leaders are appointed by God for His purposes and His purposes always work for the good of those who are His and bring major blessings to His people in due season. In the Old Testament there were kings. Some were good kings, and some were bad kings, but all the kings were appointed by God for His purposes. Even Pharaoh was raised to leadership for God to use to show His mighty power and free the slaves. God appointed Moses as leader of all of them and look what happens when they criticize and rebel against him. When his sister Miriam grumbled against him, she was struck with leprosy in Numbers, chapter 12. And again, in Numbers we find Dathan and Abiram, very popular with the people, criticize Moses and Miriam in front of another named Korah. Look what happens when God's anointed and appointed leaders are railed against. In Numbers 26:10 we find the earth opened and swallowed them along with Korah. And when that whole company of 250 men was devoured by fire, it became a sign, a warning.

We should not speak out and rebel against our leaders as we are rebelling against God and His Son, Jesus! In essence, they are the government and we will bring judgment upon ourselves in so doing. Satan rebelled against God, got himself thrown out of heaven and cursed for all eternity. Rebellion is lawlessness and witchcraft! First Samuel 15:23 shows us the true spirit of rebellion. Here, the prophet Samuel told Saul "Rebellion is as the spirit of witchcraft." Saul had only obeyed God in part, but that was viewed as totally disobedient in God's eyes. The spirit of rebellion is the spirit of witchcraft and witchcraft is the spirit of Satan.

Romans 12:1-2 "I beseech you therefore, brethren, by the mercies of God, that you present your bodies a living sacrifice, holy, acceptable to God, which is your reasonable service. And do not be conformed to this world, but be transformed by the renewing of your mind, that you may prove what is that good and acceptable and perfect will of God"

Lord Jesus, help us all not to let the spirit of rebellion into your ordained authority whether it be regarding the government, our homes, our schools, or our churches! Amen!

CHAPTER ELEVEN
PERFECT LOVE

As mentioned in chapter eight, the love Father God had for us when He planned to send His only begotten Son to redeem all mankind from our sinful state, although we were wicked, filthy, and perverse, was the perfect love. The love Jesus had for us to lay down His life so that we would not remain in that fallen wretched state, but be forgiven and receive eternal life, was perfect love. Not only perfect, but intimate as well. Let's examine perfect intimate love a little deeper.

When you think of your loved ones, your spouse, or of your children, you know and love them intimately and know things about them that others do not because of that intimacy. It is in this way that God loves us, but to an even greater immeasurable degree. One of the ways God lets us know of the deep intimate love He has for us is found in Luke 12:6. Jesus was talking about how the Father knows and values the sparrows then goes on to teach how much more the Father knows, values and loves us saying, "but the very hairs of your head are all numbered…".

Let's think about that for a moment. God knows us more intimately than we know ourselves, so intimately, that He even knows exactly how many hairs we have on our head at all times. When you finish brushing or combing your hair, the brush and comb have loosened and lost hairs in them. God knows exactly how many dropped and how many still remain. Or think of the drain cover after you bathe or shower. It has a collection of fallen hairs caught on it and again, God knows the exact count of both those hairs that have fallen and those remaining. He even is aware of the random loss of a hair that happens naturally. This is just mindboggling to me! It is an incomparable intimate love that cannot be equaled.

One example of God knowing and loving me intimately, and therefore caring for me more so than the sparrows, occurred right after Bill and I had bought a new larger home after our son was born. We had only lived there for about six months when Bill got permanently laid off from his job. He got unemployment pay and that was enough to cover all of our bills but left no money for food. We cried out to God as our pantry and refrigerator became bear.

The next thing we knew, Bill's mom came over with quite a few bags of groceries telling us her church had taken up a collection for us. Everything we needed was in those bags of groceries. We had the staples for our whole family to eat healthily for several weeks. I was so thankful! Bill also had worked some side jobs, so we were able to buy ourselves more of the basics enabling us to provide well rounded meals for ourselves and the children.

But after eating grains, cereal and bread, peanut butter, canned vegetables and fruit, potatoes, milk, eggs, cheese, and hamburger and chicken, I began to have some cravings. My two favorite snacks at that time were Cheetos for the salty craving and Oreo cookies for the sweet. I never said a word about it, not only to spare Bill feelings of inadequacy, but so as not to seem ungrateful. But those cravings seemed to grow with each passing day and though I tried to just ignore them, they seemed to pop up more and more often.

Then one evening shortly thereafter, we heard a knock on the front door. Upon answering it, we found our pastor there to drop off a big box of food. He told us the church had donated some food for the family to help take the burden off Bill as he searched for a new job. The box was full of canned goods but sitting right on top of everything was a bag of Cheetos and a package of Oreo cookies. I couldn't believe my eyes! God knew and loved me so intimately, that He gave me the desire of my heart without my uttering a word to anyone about those cravings. He loved and cared for me so much, He even provided items to relieve the cravings that were driving me crazy. That is the perfect love of the Father!

Perfect love also encompasses compassion at its very core. God calls his church, us, every member of the body of Christ, to walk in that perfect love as well. But it does not come without a price. God paid the price by sending His Son to take away our sin. It cost Him as He could not even look at His beloved Son with every sin committed by all of us from the beginning to the end, upon Him, not to mention turning away so as not to see His beloved Son in such pain and agony. It cost Jesus, when upon the cross, for the first and only time, He couldn't feel His father's loving gaze upon Him causing Him to feel abandonment. He felt all alone and deserted in that most trying moment causing Him to cry out, My God, My God, why have You forsaken Me? (Mark 15:34) Jesus is quoting the first sentence of Psalm 22 to express His deep agony on the cross. He is suffering the penalty for our sin, in our place. The consequence for sin is spiritual death. Jesus paid that awful price because He loved us with that perfect love.

God the Father and God the Son looked upon us with compassion and that compassion was the motivating factor in what they did for us. Walking in perfect love is what will cause us to look out at the dark world we live in and see the battle weary, hurt and shattered souls camouflaged beneath rough and tough, hardened and cynical exteriors. That compassion filled perfect love will move us to love on them and share the good news with them. It will cause us to see past the drug addict, prostitute, homosexual or alcoholic, and see that heart wrenching pain radiating throughout their whole being that won't release its death grip, holding their minds and hearts captive to it. It then will move us to genuinely reach out and share the love of Jesus with them in hopes they will be forgiven and set free as we are.

When is the last time we looked past the evil deeds of the kid who shot up a school and killed classmates, and saw into their breaking heart and suffering soul? When was the last time we even cared to find out what tragic abuse and rejection they must have gone through to bring them to that place? I know. Ouch! And if we're completely honest with ourselves, we'll admit that we cannot do that on our own, we need Jesus for that. We need to pray and ask God to be able to see as He does, to see through the eyes of the Father, eyes that see through a filter of love.

Let's turn to the scriptures and see what they have to say about love to gain a greater understanding of the love God desires us to walk in. It says in First Corinthians 13:4-8, "Love suffers long and is kind; love does not envy, love does not parade itself, is not puffed up, does not behave rudely, does not seek its own, is not provoked, thinks no evil, does not rejoice in iniquity, but rejoices in the truth; bears all things, hopes all things, endures all things. Love never fails…" Wow! That's a lot to take in and internalize. As I mentioned before, collectively, we are not there yet. To be able to walk in this perfect love takes battling our flesh and carnal selves on a daily basis. But God is perfecting the church to do just that. And remember, we can do all things through Christ who strengthens us.

Scripture teaches us that love covers a multitude of sins. First Peter 4:7-8 says, "But the end of all things is at hand; therefore, be serious and watchful in your prayers. And above all things have fervent love for one another, for love will cover a multitude of sins." The hurting world out there needs this from us. Proverbs 10:12 says,

"Hatred stirs up strife, but love covers all sins." Proverbs 19:11 says, "The discretion of a man makes him slow to anger, and his glory is to overlook a transgression." And this brings us back around to the love verses in First Corinthians we just discussed.

As I mentioned before, love is multi-faceted. We've discussed the love God has for us and the love He calls us to walk in and show the lost and hurting in the world. Now let's look at a different facet of our Father's love for us. The scriptures also teach us that God's love for us includes correction and chastisement. Proverbs 3:11-12 says, "My son, do not despise the chastening of the Lord, nor detest His correction; For whom the Lord loves He corrects, just as a father the son in whom he delights". Hebrews 12:11 states, "Now, no chastening seems to be joyful for the present, but painful; nevertheless, afterward it yields the peaceable fruit of righteousness to those who have been trained by it". Job 5:17 says, "Behold, happy is the man whom God corrects; therefore, do not despise the chastening of the Almighty." And Second Timothy 3:16-17 teaches us, "All scripture is given by inspiration of God and is profitable for doctrine, for reproof, for correction, for instruction in righteousness, that the man of God may be complete, thoroughly equipped for every good work."

Correction, reproof and chastisement from the Lord can come in a variety of different ways. To help you understand, I'll share a few times where I received correction from Father God myself. Once He began to have me exercise the prophetic gift He had put within me, a barrage of people from our church began to inform me of what some of the other members of our church were saying about it and me. One person told me that the pastor's wife, referring to a prophetic word I had given, said "God would never say that!" although it was scripture. Another told me that some of the women were saying that I was listening to the devil, not God, and it was spreading through the church, therefore, no one was going to come to the prayer meeting Bill and I held at our home. This sent me into a tailspin of doubt.

An intense battle was taking place in my mind where I would go from stating I knew the words were from God despite what others were saying, to wondering if I was listening to the devil since everyone else was in agreement on it, back to declaring to myself that God had used me to speak and I knew that because He had been speaking to me since I was just a little girl, to again wondering if I was being used by the devil.

Over and over the battle raged and I couldn't escape it. I couldn't think of anything else and was tormented by those opposing thoughts. Then the Lord spoke and chastised me. He said, "I am the great shepherd and My sheep know My voice! I would be greatly saddened if upon judgment day I had to say to you, take your place on my left with the other goats and prepare for the Hell fires." Let me tell you that settled it right then and there! I knew beyond a shadow of a doubt that God had been giving me those words and that I did indeed know His voice. And no matter what anyone said, I was going to speak whatever He gave me to speak.

Another time the Lord had to correct me was when Bill brought a financial decision before me. We discussed it and Bill told me to think about it. I took it to God in prayer. After praying, I got a foreboding within my spirit and knew it was not the right thing to do. When Bill brought it up again the next evening, I told him I thought it was the wrong thing to do and wouldn't be wise at this time. Apparently, he had made up his mind already and declared to me that he was going to do it anyway because he was head of the household and the end decision ultimately was his.

The next day I was praying and asked God to please not let Bill do it. I told God that I knew it was the wrong decision because He himself had given me the sick feeling in my stomach over it. I cried out to God pleading with Him and telling Him I knew we would suffer if Bill went through with it and that it just wasn't fair that I should have to suffer because of a stupid decision Bill made. The correction then came swiftly. The Lord spoke. He asked me, "And how many times has Bill had to suffer because of a stupid decision you made?" Ha! That shut me right up! I didn't understand at the time that this was something God was going to use to teach Bill and me a life lesson we had to learn to be able to go on and become what God had planned for us, to bring us to the very place we are right now.

Just very recently, God gave me a little chastisement too. It was about writing this book actually. After He had told me He wanted me to write it and told me what He wanted it about, I was hesitant because I know the Scriptures say to whom much is given, much is required as well as say, let not many of you become teachers, knowing that we shall receive a stricter judgment. These had me paralyzed in reverent fear. I wanted to be obedient and write this book as God told me to do, but I also was very cautious as how to write it and how to bring forth the principles He was showing me in times of prayer.

So, there I was, crying out to God, asking Him what exactly He wanted me to say about these things. I was asking Him how He wanted me to precisely present them. Then the chastisement came. He again answered me by asking me a question, He asked, "Sooo, what? You want me to write this book too?" That made me burst out laughing. I knew then God was telling me He had done His part by giving me what He wanted me to write about and I had to do my part in the actual writing of the book. It is He who gave me the gift of writing in the first place, after all. All the glory is His!

See, God knows us so intimately, He knows just what to say in correcting us to get through to us. Sometimes it will be stern and other times, frothed with humor. In all of the above instances where God corrected me, it was the exact way I needed at that time in order for me to understand and respond accordingly. Hallelujah! What a mighty, awesome God we serve!

I shared the above instances of correction so we would understand that God is not a father who is out to punish us, but lovingly bring us discipline, as we do with our own children. There are times He also allows us to go through some uncomfortable situations as in the above example of Bill's financial decision. God is not up in heaven with a fire thrower waiting for us to make a mistake so He can then take aim, shoot, and cause us to go through a painful fiery situation as punishment. But rather, He allows us to go through some painful situations in order to help us realize we need some correction in the course we're on. It is His heavenly global positioning system working to get us back on the right track. It is just Him "recalculating" because He loves us as His sons. We need to understand that He is also right there with us in that fiery furnace governing the flames, so we won't get burned up. Thank you, Lord, for not giving up on us and for continuing to discipline us, mold, shape and refine us, as we give more and more of ourselves to you, ever growing into maturity.

I hear the Spirit saying God is bringing His church to the place of His love and His compassion as He matures us into the bride of Christ, without spot, nor wrinkle, nor blemish of any kind for Jesus, the bridegroom. And as we walk in that love filled with compassion, His power will be manifest in a way the world has not seen before. It will be a worldwide love affair, a perfect love the likes of which today's world has not experienced. It will be the love that triumphs over hatred and fear. It will be God's perfect love radiating from us that draws people to Him. It will be His perfect love that covers a multitude of sin and brings in the great harvest, plucking people right out of the enemy's clutches.

Jesus summed up perfect love in John 15: 9-17 "As the Father loved Me, I also have loved you; abide in My love. If you keep my commandments, you will abide in My love, just as I have kept My Father's commandments and abide in His Love.

These things I have spoken to you, that My joy may remain in you, and that your joy may be full. This is my commandment, that you love one another as I have loved you. Greater love has no one than this, than to lay down one's life for his friends. You are My friends if you do whatever I command you. No longer do I call you servants, for a servant does not know what his master is doing; but I have called you friends, for all things that I heard from My Father I have made known to you. You did not choose Me, but I chose you and appointed you that you should go and bear fruit, and that your fruit should remain, that whatever you ask the Father in My name He may give you. These things I command you, that you love one another."

First John 4:18 says, "There is no fear in love; but perfect love casts out fear, because fear involves torment. But he who fears has not been made perfect in love."

May we seek to walk in God's perfect love and bring it to the lost, hurting and frightened people of the world, in Jesus' name, Amen!

CHAPTER TWELVE
OUT OF GROSS DARKNESS INTO GLORIOUS LIGHT

It's dark out there. Darkness covers the land and gross darkness, the people. It appears that Satan is gaining ground in the battle waged long ago when Satan decided in his heart to ascend in the heavens above God and got himself thrown out of heaven along with one-third of the angels who rebelled with him. But that's okay. No, really. God is in charge just as He has always been. See, Satan can only do what God allows him to do and God only allows him to work in God's own favor. When things appear the darkest, God's light shines the brightest and brings the biggest victories. Let's take a walk back through the pages of the Word of God, a stroll down Scripture Memory Lane and see.

We'll start with Job. The Bible tells us that Satan was roaming the earth looking for someone to devour and sets his sight on Job. Satan appeared before God and had the audacity to question Job's faithfulness to God. God says, "Sure, you can test him. I give you permission. Everything Job has is now in your power, but you cannot touch Job himself." Notice God is the one who made the rules and set the boundaries for Job's struggle.

Job wins that round and then Satan complains and whines to God expressing the only reason Job won was because he wasn't forced to experience pain in his body. So, God again allowed Satan permission and again set the parameters. God said, "Okay then, Job is in your power, but you mustn't take his life."

Job wins again in the end and his faith and health are stronger than ever. He ends up with more than everything he had to begin with and lost. He ends up more blessed than when this all started and received a double portion. Satan has no power except that which God allows. And God allows it only for our good! Yes, Satan still has to serve God. Satan is just a tool in God's control. Give God praise!

Let's walk further back down Scripture Memory Lane and look at Moses. You can just imagine Satan, hands raised and clasped together in victory when God's chosen deliverer of his people, people who had been held in bondage for 400 years, is banished out of Egypt into the deadly desert. Satan didn't realize it was there God would shape Moses and he would be forged into a leader.

You can even visualize Satan snickering when Moses

becomes a lowly shepherd of sheep. Again, Satan didn't realize this was training for God's purpose, the very training Moses needed to lead a people out of bondage into the Promised Land. Nor did Satan know that while in the role of sheep herder, Moses would come face to face with the living God through a burning bush and receive the instructions to set God's people free.

Or how about in the book of Daniel when Daniel was thrown into the lion's den and the youth, Shadrach, Meshach and Abednego were thrown into the fiery furnace while King Nebuchadnezzar continued to be troublesome to God's people by forbidding them to worship God and commanding that they worship his idol? In the end, Nebuchadnezzar praised and honored God, proclaiming God's works as truth and His ways just. Again, and again, we see Satan as just a pawn in God's plan.

Now let's speed forward up Scripture Memory Lane and take a look at Peter. Jesus gives him a warning and says, "Simon, Simon! Indeed, Satan has asked for you that he may sift you as wheat. But I have prayed for you, that your faith should not fail; and when you have returned to Me, strengthen your brethren."

This is another example of Satan having a plan against one of God's servants but having to ask permission to do so. It's also another example of Satan's plan working into the plan of God as well. God's purpose for allowing this test was to mold, shape and mature Peter and to make available a testimony for the church. After the trial, when Peter returned, he encouraged his brothers. Peter's account now serves as a testimony to us all. Know that whatever trials we go through, God is there to help us from beginning to end and cause us to be a living testimony of His power; of how He brought us out of the darkness and into the light.

And that is all that is happening now in the land. Division is everywhere. Sin abounds and leaders snub their noses at the Almighty God. They pass laws making the very sin that God hates, legal for the people, bringing them into bondage all the while, declaring to them that they are free, free to do what makes their flesh, their carnal nature, themselves, feel good. The exact same thing the enemy tempts us with. They encourage you to satisfy your flesh also known as your sin nature, snubbing your nose at your spirit-self. Many schools forbid prayer and the mention of God and His Son, Jesus in classrooms. Sexual confusion and identity crisis abound. Drug addiction, alcoholism and depression are at all-time highs. Little girls are cutting themselves to bring physical pain in hopes to override the mental and emotional pain they experience. Killing unborn babies is legal. I'll stop right there. You get the picture as we've already discussed some of this in previous chapters.

Yes, there is gross darkness out there, but only because God is allowing Satan to work evil. It's only for an appointed time though and will bring about another great victory for heaven. God's always in charge and is doing a new thing in this darkness, just as He always has when darkness has covered the land. God is pouring out new anointing, preparing to use children/youth to confound the wise, stepping up the ministry of angels, and bringing about supernatural manifestations as signs, as we go out as laborers into the fields to harvest.

He has been preparing, building, teaching and maturing his church line upon line and precept upon precept for over 2000 years. He has been doing it for such a time as this. He is preparing to shine in this gross darkness. You see, God's light shines the brightest in gross darkness. Philippians 2:14-15 "Do all things without grumbling or questioning, that you may be blameless and innocent, children of God without blemish in the midst of a crooked and perverse generation, among whom you shine as lights in the world." Rejoice! We, His children, are children of purpose! We are forgiven and not forgotten! Let us go forth and show this truth to the world!

The Lord gave me a vision as He was explaining how we shine as lights in the world and what is going to be happening as we, the carriers of His light, share it with the world. He showed me a visualization of the earth that reminded me of the satellite pictures of the earth at night, from up in space. It was His bird's eye view from up in the heavenlies. In the big cities there were pockets of very bright lights. There were also clusters of smaller areas of lights. These clusters were mainly on the outskirts of the continents, and along the shores of the oceans. He explained to me that those clusters were His people bearing His light, congregated together.

He then brought my attention to pin pricks of light sparsely dispersed here and there in otherwise dark areas, explaining these were His people who had come out from the larger clusters into the varying regions, sharing their testimonies of what He has done in their lives. He then said He was asking His people to come out from their churches and go out into their communities and regions and beyond, via many and varied methods, proclaiming what He had done for them and will do for others. It will be much like the wedding feast in Matthew 22:9 when the king said to his servants, "Therefore go into the highways and as many as you find, invite to the wedding."

He then told me to watch and see what happens. Those pin pricks of light then began moving and soon were transformed into larger clusters too, all of which continued moving and increasing in size. The earth became illuminated, brightly glowing with a significant reduction of darkness. He then continued and explained that as His people moved out sharing, He was combining supernatural manifestations throughout the earth in conjunction with the words of His people. There are going to be supernatural manifestations such as the world has not experienced before. All of the darkness was not eradicated however, and He explained there was a future time and purpose appointed for that. Nonetheless, the combination of God's supernatural power and His people's words going forth was causing the increase. Hallelujah!

Later, as I was praying and seeking Him, I heard the Spirit of the Lord say to me, "It is the time of the dueling roaring lions." He gave me the scriptures First Peter 5:8 "Be sober, be vigilant; because your adversary the devil walks about like a roaring lion, seeking whom he may devour", and Revelation 5:5 where Jesus is referred to as the Lion of Judah.

I understood that both Jesus and the devil were referred to as lions but were opposing forces. My brain chewed and chewed on this for a few days and I couldn't escape the comparison. So, I began praying asking God to reveal more of what He was saying as I knew there was more he wanted me to comprehend.

In further prayer and seeking, God gave me the following scriptures and brought clarity to what he was saying. Revelation 12:12 "…for the devil has come down to you, having great wrath, because he knows he has a short time."

Next He gave me Hosea 11:10 "They shall walk after the Lord. He will roar like a lion. When He roars, Then His sons shall come trembling from the west."

He then gave me Amos 1:2 "…the Lord roars from Zion."

He followed this with Amos 3:7-8 "Surely the Lord God does nothing unless He reveals His secret to His servants the prophets. A lion has roared! Who will not fear? The Lord God has spoken! Who can but prophesy?"

It became clear at this time that the time of the dueling roaring lions refers to both of their final harvests. The devil is roaring seeking to take and keep captive all that he can before his short time is up. At the same time, Jesus is roaring as well, that time is short and soon will gather his final harvest. He is calling for His prophets in the meantime to proclaim this to the people and for His people to go out and reap this great harvest, to bring many out of the darkness and into His glorious light.

Revelation 14:14-20 tells us of the impending dual harvests and reads, "Then I looked, and behold, a white cloud, and on the cloud sat One like the Son of Man, having on His head a golden crown, and in His hand a sharp sickle. And another angel came out of the temple, crying with a loud voice to Him who sat on the cloud, 'Thrust in Your sickle and reap, for the time has come for You to reap, the harvest of the earth is ripe.' So, He who sat on the cloud thrust in His sickle on the earth, and the earth was reaped.

Then another angel came out of the temple, which is in heaven, he also having a sharp sickle.

And another angel came out from the altar, who had power over fire, and he cried with a loud cry to him who had the sharp sickle, saying, 'Thrust in your sharp sickle and gather the clusters of the vine of the earth, for her grapes are fully ripe.' So, the angel thrust his sickle into the earth and gathered the vine of the earth and threw it into the great winepress of the wrath of God. And the winepress was trampled outside the city, and blood came out of the winepress, up to the horses' bridles, for one thousand six hundred furloughs."

The final harvests are coming, but they are not yet. The lions are still roaring. It says in Amos 3:4 "Will a lion roar in the forest, when he has no prey?" When a lion is roaring, it is warning of its presence and that it is on the prowl. If there were no more to harvest, the lion would not roar. So, as we look out into the world and see all of the iniquity abounding, all of the darkness seizing people's hearts, we see Satan still going about roaring, looking for whom he can devour. And as we see all of the scary things happening right now, taking place all over the earth, in every single country, we know that Jesus, the Lion of Judah, is still roaring as well, calling upon His people to carry His light into the darkness and bring hope to a floundering, lost, scared, and searching people. God is still calling and seeking many to come to Him and become His children.

I heard the Spirit say, "There is yet to be the great harvest and right now I am preparing the fields. Before any harvest can be reaped, the fallow ground must be broken up. It must be so, so that My seeds may be planted. Once My seeds are planted, they must be watered and fed till they are ripe for the harvest in their due season, then the great harvest comes. Fear not nor be dismayed for I am now preparing the fields by breaking up the fallow ground."

Thank you, Father! This is the season of breaking up the fallow ground! It is a season of hope and joy and your people should not fear but rejoice! Job 3:25 teaches "For the thing I greatly feared has come upon me…" Do not be afraid, but trust in God and rest in His presence and His peace, says the Lord!

Will you follow him and let your love light shine, let Him teach you and build you up to be a strong vessel of light? Will you let your light shine for Him and help usher in freedom to the masses held in bondage to the darkness of carnal self and the gross darkness upon the people?

In Luke chapter 10:2 Jesus said, "The harvest truly is great, but the laborers are few; therefore, pray the Lord of the harvest to send out laborers into His harvest." May we be like Isaiah in Isaiah 6:8 and answer the question the Lord asks, "Whom shall I send and who will go for Us?" with "Here am I, send me!"

Other titles from Higher Ground Books & Media:

Wise Up to Rise Up by Rebecca Benston

A Path to Shalom by Steen Burke

For His Eyes Only by John Salmon, Ph.D.

Miracles: I Love Them by Forest Godin

32 Days with Christ's Passion by Mark Etter

The Bottom of This by Tramaine Hannah

Saved by a Mystery by Deborah Randall

Out of Darkness by Stephen Bowman

Breaking the Cycle by Willie Deeanjlo White

Healing in God's Power by Yvonne Green

Chronicles of a Spiritual Journey by Stephen Shepherd

The Real Prison Diaries by Judy Frisby

My Name is Sam…And Heaven is Still Shining Through by Joe Siccardi

Add these titles to your collection today!

http://www.highergroundbooksandmedia.com

Do you have a story to tell?

Higher Ground Books & Media is an independent Christian-based publisher specializing in stories of triumph! Our purpose is to empower, inspire, and educate through the sharing of personal experiences.

Please visit our website for our submission guidelines.

http://www.highergroundbooksandmedia.com

Made in the USA
Coppell, TX
07 February 2021

49592774R00059